# Zen of Zinn 2

## More Wisdom from Silicon Valley's Longest Serving CEO

## by Ray Zinn

ISBN: 9798737291938

Library of Congress Cataloging-in-Publication Data Zinn, Ray.

Zen of Zinn 2: More Wisdom from Silicon Valley's Longest Serving CEO / Ray Zinn.

1.  Leadership. 2. Culture. 3. Entrepreneurship.


COVER DESIGN: Heidi Springer, Grace Design Studios

ILLUSTRATIONS: John Smillie

# Contents

# Foreword

From border-state cattle ranch to Silicon Valley. From hard scrabble living to high-tech CEO.

That has been my life, and a life well lived. You cannot cover that much time and territory without learning much about people, business, society, humanity, discipline and love for your fellow man.

*Zen of Zinn 2* (and its predecessor *Zen of Zinn*) distills this lifetime of acquired knowledge and wisdom so that you, the kind reader, do not have to stub your toes on the rocky road called life.

   –   Ray Zinn

# Management, Entrepreneurship and Leadership

There is an old adage, "measure twice and cut once".

In our busy lives, we sometimes don't take the time to do things right. We get in too big a hurry. We somehow believe that we are going to be lucky and that everything will turn out right without having to do the extra work of validating our assumptions. When we end up not being lucky, we just say, "well no one is perfect".

Save yourself a lot of heartache and woe by taking the appropriate time to insure you are going to have a good outcome.

If you think you're smart, you're probably not.

Smart people are humble people and don't need to show off their intelligence. They know who they are and what they can do. They are good listeners, not talkers.

Who is more important, employees, customers, or stakeholders?

This is like asking, what is more important your arms, your legs, or your head. They are work together for the betterment of the company. For without each of them, you will not have a successful enterprise.

Interestingly enough, they all have a "stake" in the company and thus are all stakeholders. Treat all three equally and you will have a well-balanced company.

The best dogsled teams have a good leader. It is the lead dog that keeps the rest of the team moving succinctly.

Likewise, great companies have great leaders. They keep the team together and moving in the right direction. They do not bark out their instructions – they use quiet but firm examples of where the team should go.

Be a good leader not a good barker.

We have all heard the expression, " if at first you don't succeed, try, try again".

This comes with a caveat.

Repeating the same mistake and expecting a different result is insanity. When we try, try again, we need to learn from our mistakes and not repeat them.

Persistence is the glue that keeps you stuck. Knowledge is the solvent that sets you free.

We need to think slower but act quickly.

I know this sounds like an oxymoron but the way our brains are wired, thinking quickly is important to get us out of a dire situation. This quick sizing up capability works well under these emergency situations when fast action is required. Unfortunately, it can cause problems if sudden reactions are not required and these actions make us jump to the wrong conclusion.

Another aspect of a rush to judgement is when the artifact of the conclusion we draw meets our expectation. In other words, our bias decides for us before all of the facts are in.

If time is not of the essence, think more slowly before reacting to the situation. Do a proper job of due diligence: fact check.

Why do we panic during a crisis? In a word it is "fear".

Most of us are risk averse. We fear the unknown. Just place a blindfold on someone even in a familiar place and when you ask them to move, their hands immediately stretch out in front of them and they move very slowly.

This is how we deal with crises. We put on the brakes and slow down. There is no solution to this. It is just natural. We are just fearful when things happen around us that we can't explain or understand.

To minimize the panic mode and help others deal with the crisis, we need to calm ourselves so that we don't overreact and enhance the crisis making it worse. Calmness helps us deal with crises thus helping minimize the effects of the crisis.

Getting it right is the key for a successful outcome.

However, getting it right the first time is not easy. It goes to the saying "measure twice and cut once". Unfortunately, getting it right the first time requires knowledge in areas we don't always have.

This is where we need to depend on the experts. Most importantly, make sure they are trusted experts.

You can't always depend on YouTube.

Trying to  start a company is like playing Russian roulette with 5 of 6 chambers loaded.

Statistics show that 9 out of 10 startups fail within the first three years. To beat these odds there are four classes you need to take: basic accounting, financial and managerial accounting, business law, and basic economics.

Studies show that most employees quit their jobs because they don't like or get along with their supervisor.

When you then start the job search, how do you know if you will get along or like your new supervisor? Here are some thoughts. Most of us can get along with almost anyone. However, there are some bosses that are just plain difficult. They can be just plain mean, condescending, demanding, obnoxious, and inconsiderate.

The best way to determine what kind of supervisor your new boss will be is to talk to a number of those that currently or in the past worked for him or her. If that is not possible, then during the interview, get their view on certain key issues important to you. You can generally tell during the interview if you are going to hit it off. Ask yourself, would I like to be friends with this person? If yes, then you are likely to get along.

During the days of horse drawn carriages (buggies), "buggy whips" was a huge and thriving industry that lasted over 100 years. Then came along the automobiles, which negated horses and buggies for transportation. This killed the buggy whip industry almost overnight.

Change is always with us. The book "Who Moved the Cheese" talks about mice who were so programmed to return to the same spot every night for cheese, that when the cheese was moved from their favorite spot, they couldn't adapt and thus starved to death.

Accepting and adjusting to change is key to maintaining a thriving business over the long-term. Don't get caught looking for the cheese in the same spot or risk starving to death. Prepare now for change and don't wait until your cheese is moved.

"Go for broke" means to risk everything.

When I started my company, Micrel, we risked everything since we funded the company with our own money.

I am often asked to invest in startups. The first question I always ask is " How much do you or will you have invested in your startup?". If they are not willing to "Go for broke", I am not interested in the rest of their pitch.

Sometimes we seem to have more solutions than problems.

This happens when we think there is a problem when there really isn't one, and that can be dangerous. As the saying goes, "if it ain't broke, don't fix it".

The perception that there is a problem, becomes the problem. We can become so fixated on an issue that we create a problem. This especially happens in relationships.

Don't conjure up a problem that really isn't there. Great harm can result.

Silos. Sigh.

All of us need to establish our own identity. It says who we are and what we stand for. Company teams, military teams, or for that matter sports teams, are no exception.

Teams work together to perform certain job functions. Their identity defines this job function. The downside to this is that teams tend to form silos. It is natural and protects their identity. This good news, bad news situation has to be carefully monitored or the intra-functional relationships will suffer.

The tighter the functional identities are, the more likely silos will form, and this is a very important downside to consider and work around.

Strong team identifies with good intra-functional relationships is ideal. To combat the tendency toward erecting silos is to have intra-functional team identify work toward the common cause. Here is where having a strong corporate culture with a clearly defined mission is crucial.

Want to master the art of being successful? There are three basic steps.

1.  Read my bestselling book, Tough Things First .

2.  Master the art of problem solving. Look for a need and fill it. There are always ways to improve our lives. Not everything has been invented. The next invention is just waiting for you to come up with it.

3.  Master the art of team building. Finding the right team is a matter of finding people who share your dream and then keeping them excited and motivated.

"When all else fails, read the instructions." This saying has bugged me forever. Why do we try to do things without understanding the task? Is it that we are stubborn or lazy? Maybe both?

At Micrel, a company I ran for 37 years, we had a very detailed policy and procedures manual. The purpose for these was to ensure compliance, uniformity, and consistency across the company. Yet, I found that some employees neither read nor followed the procedures even though we tried to make the procedures simple, short, and logical.

Of course, we didn't discover the fact that an employee was not following the procedures until we had a problem. Even if the employees had read the P&Ps at one time, there was no guarantee that they would remember what they read.

For important policies and procedures, it is necessary to have them read and re-read regularly, perhaps every few months. If company policies and procedures are important, you must ensure that the pertinent employees know, understand, and follow them or else they will be deemed worthless.

Start by keeping your policies and procedures short, easy to understand, and to the point.

Ministering and administering are two words that sound similar but are very different. "Ministering" is the loving care for others. "Administering" is the supervision or managing of a task or function. The trick is to combine the two to get the best results.

If we can supervise or manage in a loving, caring way, just think how wonderful our workplaces, home, and communities would be.

Leadership is more than just delegating and managing work assignments. The primary goal of leadership is to inspire and motivate.

Inspiring and motivating is a tireless and sometimes thankless responsibility. It requires numerous acts of kindness and being a willing listener. People will follow a leader they love and respect; not fear.

In my book, Tough Things First, I discuss the four main attributes of a good leader.

1. Honesty: You can always count on them being truthful even if it hurts them. They are ruthlessly transparent: they leave out nothing.

2. Integrity: They do what is right even when no one is watching.  Their morals are based on righteous principles and not on what is politically correct or in fashion. They have a reputation of being decent, good, and above all, law abiding.

3. They respect the dignity and rights of all people: They are not given to using vulgar or condescending language. They treat everyone with love and fairness.

4. They always do whatever it takes, no excuses: You can count on them to meet their commitments. If they make a mistake, they fix it. They do not blame others.

These are the kind of people you want as leaders. They are not only dependable, but they also lead by example. They have your back and you can trust them.

To improve your decision making, check your gut.

If it doesn't feel right, it is probable the wrong decision. Good decisions usually feel right in your gut.

Just like in sports, the ability to "pivot" is very important for running a successful business. While at Micrel, a semiconductor company, we had to pivot 10 times in the 37 years I ran the company. This is an average of one pivot every 3-4 years.

Not being able to pivot accounts for why so many companies, large and small, fail. Even large well-established companies like Radio Shack, Toys "R" Us, K Mart, and so many others have had to close up shop because they just couldn't "pivot".

So how does a company learn to pivot? Pivoting is a cultural thing. It has to be built into the DNA of the company in the beginning. There has to be a vision of pivoting. In the book, "Who Moved the Cheese", the author talks about the need to pivot or die.

Whether you are the leader of a company or an employee, you need to explore and understand the company's pivoting strategy. Remember, "learn to pivot or die".

While running Micrel, which I did for 37 years, I always reinforced the importance of customer service with my employees. It is important. When you look at online customer reviews, they primarily complain about quality and customer service.

Bad customer service trumps almost any positive product attribute.  You can make a great product and lose the customer with lousy service. Likewise, good customer service and support can overcome many product problems and issues.

Treat the customer right and you will have them forever.

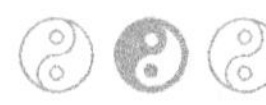

A "bad" CEO is usually a bad person. They may be well connected and competent business-wise but are not good personal examples and in the ways that they lead and treat people.

To the contrary, a "good" CEO  may not be loved by Wall Street but is loved by his or her people. They are honest and ethically beyond reproach. They are never condescending or use foul language.  They are good examples to all.

The prescriptions for a healthy company are important. Here are some ideas to have a healthy company.

1. Have at least 3 months of working capital(cash) on hand at all times.
2. Maintain a healthy culture: honesty, integrity, respect for all persons, and doing what it takes – no excuses.
3. Avoid using any condescending language:  vulgar language.
4. Hold regular all-hands meetings to communicate the company's health. Be totally transparent.
5. Be kind and benevolent.
6. Be completely fair and show no favoritism.
7. Don't pressure your employees to work long hours.

One sign of a true leader is the ability to love others without the need to be loved in return. This is a pillar of servant leadership.

Servant leaders are meek, not weak. Being meek means you don't act like you know it all. You are not caught up in yourself. You are easily imposed upon,  meaning you are always willing to help. You are also a good listener.

You gain the love and respect of your people when they know they can trust you. You are not just their boss; you are their friend.

"Pride proceeded the fall." This ancient saying goes back thousands of years. Dynasties, kingdoms, nations, and civilizations have fallen due to pride. "Pride" is an inward focused characteristic. It is the exact opposite of humility. Once you think you know it all, the end is near.

When a confident CEO – or for that matter any leader – succumbs to hubris (having excessive pride in oneself), they are doomed and will likely fall. Fight "pride" like it is one of your worst enemies.

Diversity can be tough, but it helps us grow.

At Micrel, we had a very diverse workforce. As it was for Micrel, diversity can be great when you are prepared to deal with cultural, language, habits, and differing work ethics and styles.

It is all about adapting and acceptance. If you have the right attitude about this, diversity will strengthen your company and other relationships.

"Chasing your tail" means you are running in circles. This happens when you don't have a good plan. If you fail to plan, you plan to fail.

So how do you know when you have a good plan? When as you are executing the plan, everything you are hoping for is coming together. By checking your plan frequently, you can make the necessary course corrections to stay on your plan and thus avoid endlessly circling yourself.

A breatharian is a person who appears to live on nothing but air. In business, it refers to a person whose survival is amazing. They manage to keep their business going with little or no money or other resources. They are frugal to a fault.

We need more breatharian-like CEO's running companies focused on profitability rather than just market valuation. Real companies make money.

I recently had a meeting with the CEO of a startup. He said, "you never had to go through tough times".

Knowing where this was heading, I quipped, "What makes you think I never went through tough times?" His reply was very thought provoking: "You were always profitable."

I replied, "What makes you think that being profitable isn't tough to do?" He apologized and changed his comment to, "If you are profitable, you don't have to keep raising money to stay alive." I said, "Now you're talking."

Running out of money is really tough. But running a continuously profitable business is also tough and a far better form of toughness.

I was asked by an ex-student who was seeking an executive position within his company what attributes he will need to

get this promotion. Here is the list of executive skills I
provided him.

- Jumps right in without being asked. Always willing to
  go the extra mile.

- Early to work, last one to leave.

- Doesn't take long lunch breaks.

- Doesn't whine or complain.

- Is loved by his or her people.

- Gets things done on time and lowest cost.

- Doesn't ask for anything, puts others first.

- Is kind and understanding.

- Good listener.

- Has all the attributes of the Scout Law.

- Clean shaven and well dressed.

- Lastly, does the Tough Things First.

I want to emphasize the importance of being a good example
of a humble servant who truly wants to serve rather than
being served. Too often leaders are more focused on the job

they want us to do rather than helping us with the job they want us to tackle.

The focus of a humble servant-leader is finding how to help, not just adding to our already burdensome lives.

The three key tools for becoming a successful entrepreneur are create, innovate, and negotiate.

- Create: come up with novel approaches to solve a problem.

- Innovate: overcome the sundry problems that beset every venture.

- Negotiate: getting the best possible deal to improve your chances for success.

In this light, we are all entrepreneurs even though we may not be running a company. To be successful in life, we all need to think entrepreneurially. We all need to create, innovate and negotiate.

Why do we wait until the horses get out before we close the gate?

This adage is an artifact of human nature, that we tend not to take action until a serious problem has occurred. Unfortunately, most serious problems are unique and implementing a solution that might fix any particular problem may, in fact, have unintended consequences. Or worse still, we might implement a solution for a "one off" incident that may never happen again. This is why it is important to properly identify the cause of the problem in the first place.

Too often there is rush to judgment and we cause more problems than we fix. Problem solving is an art. It requires a calm approach with a clear understanding of the root cause of the problem – the disease, not just the symptoms.

In hiring, it is all about the interview. This applies to the interviewer as well as the interviewee.

Is the individual dressed appropriate for the position?
Are they well groomed?
Is the interview conducted in an appropriate setting?
Does the individual seem warm and inviting?
Are the questions/answers appropriate for the position?
Was the individual polite and interested?
At the end of the interview, did you come away excited or concerned?

Bottom line, you need to feel the interview went well and there was a sufficient connection made. Is this individual right for you either as a boss or applicant? Your gut will usually be right.

I am often asked, what criteria do I use in deciding on a startup investment. Some of the things I look for:

- The success history of the founders must have a good track record. You don't want to invest with folks that haven't done well in previous ventures. While they usually have, in their minds, a good reason for the failure, it was not their fault. Stay away from these guys. Better safe than sorry.

- The valuation for a startup with no revenue is tricky. Make sure the reward matches the risk. I don't invest in pre-revenue startups unless I am convinced, they are generating revenue within 6 months.

- Give them a chance to talk about the challenges they face. If they focus on the problems their product solves, this is a sign of a poorly thought-out strategy.

- I look for opportunities to win. If they focus more on the need for money, they are too desperate.

- I look for companies that have sustainability. If they look like they are just trying to survive, they are most likely a money sink not a money maker.

- I look for companies that are raising enough money to take them to profitability. Otherwise, they will be spending too much time constantly raising money and not running the company.

- I only invest in startups where the founders have personally put up a sizable amount of their own money.

- I also bear in mind that 9 out of 10 startups fail within the first 3 years. Odds are not in your favor so be careful and diligent in your due diligence.

Sexual harassment is a form of sexual discrimination and is illegal in the United States. Sexual harassment is harassment (typically involving a woman) in the workplace, other professional settings or social events involving unwanted sexual advances or obscene remarks.

In the 37 years of running Micrel, we did have a number of circumstances involving charges relating to sexual harassment and/or sexual discrimination. While these charges are often difficult to prove, we dealt with them promptly and appropriately. The real key is dealing with them promptly and honestly. If the charges involved a woman(s) we always had a female in HR take the lead in the investigation.

In most cases, we found the charges to be legitimate and appropriate action was taken including termination. When the charges were not brought to our attention promptly by the victim, it caused two main problems. First, it was difficult to prove the charges because too much time had elapsed and second, it brought into question who was the real victim.

Bottomline, as a company leader, you should deal with all such charges quickly and honestly. If you are a victim, report such charges promptly and honestly just like you expect the company to do for you.

It has been my experience that most companies have a zero tolerance for such illicit behavior, and these are the types of companies you should want to work for. If you are experiencing sexual harassment or discrimination where you currently work and your company is not taking your charges seriously, you should leave or remove yourself as soon as possible from the situation. Don't assume things are going to

improve or change: report the infringement, see how the
company reacts and handles the problem and then be
prepared to leave. It is not worth the fight that will ensue.

Wise people never set sail on ships that are not seaworthy; it is
a smarter person who gets off the ship before it sinks.  This
saying is true regarding marriage, investments, and business
ventures.

Being wise has two components: first, is to know what you are
getting into and the second, is to feel it in your gut.  Such "gut
instincts" are more rational than they sound and actually have
some biological science to validate them.

Whenever you have to make a critical decision, asking
yourself "do I fully understand what I am getting into", then
sit back and ponder the decision, how do you feel about it?  If
you believe you fully understand the pros and cons and you
feel good about the choice, then proceed.  If on the other hand,
you feel you have not fully comprehended the pros and cons
and you can't truly feel right or good about the choice, then
stop, do not proceed.

Know your ship before you set sail and you will be the
happier for it.

Often, we focus so much on being solution-oriented that we
create "solutions" for which there is no real problem. This can
create more problems to solve. The old adage, "if it ain't broke
don't fix it "truly applies here.

When fixated in this way, the solution becomes the real problem. Trying to fix things that aren't really broken only makes matters worse – breaks things in new and often unexpected ways.

This brings me to my point. Defining the problem is the real issue. Too often we think there is a problem when there is not, and scurry around devising solutions only to make matters worse.

It takes a real talent to define problems correctly, so we don't come up with immaterial fixes. For example, we had a serious mice problem at the ranch and our solution was to put out numerous mouse traps. We validated the fact that we indeed had a serious mouse problem because we trapped lots of mice for a long time. So, putting out lots of mouse traps didn't stop the mouse problem.

The real problem as it turned out was leaving open containers of food around for the mice to feed on. This just encouraged more mice to come. Once we sealed up all the containers, guess what? No more mice came.

Properly defining the problem will always result in a better solution.

The phrase, "taking the long way around" means to avoid shortcuts. Shortcuts are faster but come with some risk.

Taking the long way around is a good option for the inexperienced. Those who are familiar with a shortcut can easily navigate through the process. Others, who don't feel as comfortable, avoid the shortcut because of the risk of failure.

But shortcuts need to be explored. If you never try the shortcut, you will never learn its benefits and thus will always take the long way around. People who fall into this category are risk adverse.

My suggestion is try taking some shortcuts and learn to navigate risk.

A recent study by Columbia University has shown that working more than 40 hours per week is as bad for your health as smoking. Additionally, the study revealed that only 4 hours of the workday was actually productive. The balance of the day was spent surfing the web or other such non-work-related activities.

While mine was not a university/scientifically run study, I noted similar types of activities while as the CEO of my company which I ran for 37 years. Employees can only focus for short periods of time, typically in in 1–2-hour spurts.

Leaders and managers who understand and appreciate this limitation can organize their projects to take this into account and get more productivity from their people. My strategy was to train my managers to focus on doing the tough things first each day while the employees are fresh. This improved the overall company efficiency by 20%. Thus, we didn't need to force or require our people to work more than 40 hours per week.

Sexual abuse is getting a lot of public attention as of late. The question, in my mind is, what is actual sexual abuse? Definition of "sexual abuse" is a statutory offense that provides that it is a crime to knowingly cause another person to engage in an unwanted sexual act by "force" or "threat". Statutory is usually referred to a law or being legally defined.

The issue of "sexual abuse" appears to have been widened to include any unwanted act (verbal or physical) that could be perceived by another as "sexual" in nature. This could include such physical acts as hugging, a handshake, a kiss on the cheek or hand, putting your arm around their shoulder, etc. Verbally, this could include any comments referring to their physical being, off-colored jokes or comments, offensive pictures, etc. While none of these meet the legal definition of "sexual abuse", they none the less can cause one to be accused as a "sexual abuser".

Bottom line, you may not go to jail or lose a lawsuit over these non-legal sexual abuse allegations, but you may run afoul of the press over these allegations.

Be careful with whom you get close to or you just might be fingered as a sexual abuser.

# Serving Others

To share a loving and peaceful existence requires everyone to think of others before themselves.

Sharing or giving back is a sign of gratitude. We all have benefited in some way from the efforts of others. Be grateful and willing to help others along the way. You will be happier for it.

Anytime you can give back, you win. All of the great accomplishments you achieve in the world will not amount to a hill of beans when compared to the time you spend in the service of others.

The two basic human attributes that affect our decisions are guilt and greed.

We can look at guilt as being the absence of greed and greed being the absence of guilt. They work independently of each other and never coexist. For example, guilt motivates us to be compassionate and greed removes compassion from the equation.

Greed is inward facing and  drives our decisions to acquire things like work, recreation, food, etc. While on the other hand, guilt is outward facing and drives our decisions to help others.

King Solomon, of the Old Testament, said that "life is vanity." In his case he meant it was "futile".

Solomon had it all: wealth, fame, and prestige. He had almost everything wonderful that life has to offer and yet he felt his life was futile.

Is King Solomon, right? No.

If, like King Solomon, your focus is on yourself and the gain you are expecting to get, life will be futile. This is because you cannot satisfy your appetite for life with the pleasures of the world. This is not true happiness.

True happiness comes from going outside yourself and helping others. Don't let your life be futile. Live your life for others and you will be the happier for it.

True happiness can only come from selfless service to others.

A recent study showed that the gift giver had a longer lasting feeling of joy and happiness than the gift receiver.

As the saying goes, "'tis better to give than to receive".

When life seems dark and dreary, and you feel all is lost, try losing yourself in serving others who may feel like you do.

Lifting them up, lifts you up. You will become the servant, not the victim. It is life changing to go outside yourself and help others.

Letting them feel your love fills your life with happiness and joy. Soon you will feel that life is not so dismal.

If "no good deed goes unpunished, then the Scouts would be in very bad shape since the Scout motto say to "do a good turn daily".

Though it is unlikely that a good deed might result in punishment, it is true that good deeds require some sacrifice. If we look at sacrificing as a punishment, none of us would ever want to do anything nice for anyone. But the two – sacrifice and punishment – are very different things.

It all depends on how we view our efforts. Sacrificing our time and resources to help others without thought of compensation is noble. Giving of our time and resources reluctantly is viewing your good deed as a punishment, and that is a selfish attitude.

Be noble, give willingly and often and life will be so much the merrier.

The best medicine to fight the seeds of loneliness and depression is to work in the service of others.

This medicine will inoculate you against those things that will, in part, tend to destroy you. Serving others will bring you peace and happiness. Let peace and happiness fill your soul through your selfless service of others.

When you value others, you add value to yourself. This is the surest way to improve your relationships. Looking for the good in others will help you see their value. It is like putting money in a savings account. It is always growing interest and the overall value is increased.

We are all familiar with the story, "The Genie and the Magic Lamp". In the story, the person who possess the Magic Lamp is given three wishes that the Genie will grant without reservation or hesitation.

If you possessed the Magic Lamp, what would you wish for? Would you wish for things that primarily bless you or would you wish for things that would bless others? If you would use your Magic Lamp to bless others, you are a blessed and loving person.

But wait, you possess that Magic Lamp already. Your Magic Lamp is called serving others.

We are encumbered daily with useless cares that defocus us from things that truly matter.

Usually, these useless matters are self-centered and prevent us from being of service of others. To become sincerely enriched and filled with meaningful experiences, you must drive those useless cares from your life.

Don't become a victim of your own creation. Instead become a tool to help others that are the real victims.

No one is so rich that they won't ever need help. By the same token, no one is so poor that they cannot offer help.

Giving and receiving help is a blessing to the giver and receiver. Both benefit because service is involved.

Overcoming the need for greed is a worthwhile endeavor.

Most of us have far more than we need. It has been said that seeking for more than we need is "greed" and wanting more than we have earned is "coveting". Both greed and coveting drive us to do things we will ultimately regret. They are counter to being a loving and generous person. It is focusing on being inward and not outward.

We cannot be truly happy unless we turn our focus outward: forgetting ourselves for the good of others.

"Success" is not spelled "m-o-n-e-y". Too many of us feel that "success" is equated with wealth. Far from it! "Success" is equated with accomplishment, not wealth. Overcoming "failure" is true "success".

Be a real "success" and serve your fellowman.

The Scout motto is "to do a good turn daily". I can't think of a more befitting way to start a New Year than to commit to doing a good turn for others each day of our lives.

Being of service to others is a sure way of developing more love and understanding of our fellowman. In this divisive world we live in, I can't think of anything needed more than this.

# Diligence and Determination

Don't wait for success, create it.

Emerson said that "persistence" is the key to success.

What stops many of us from succeeding is that we give up too easily. Nothing is easy except giving up.

Most successful people have had to overcome tremendous odds. They just declare that failure is not an option. They never ever give up.

Remember this simple phrase: persistence overcomes resistance.

To harden metal harder, it has to undergo a reformation process called forging. In forging, the metal is exposed to a tortuous environment of tremendous heat and hammering over and over and then quickly cooled called quenching. If this is not done in a precise manner, the metal will not become useful.

If we are to become useful, we too must go through a similar tempering process. It is through these raging fires of adversity that makes us stronger and more valuable.

Rather than complaining about the fires of adversity, accept them as good and valuable ways of strengthening. "Learn to love the things you hate and do the Tough Things First".

When you are afraid to try for fear of losing or failing, you will most likely fail to succeed at anything.

Life is full of ups and downs, highs and lows. We all love the highs but not the lows.

But reflect on this. We learn so much more from the lows than we do from the highs. It is the lows that enhance success and makes us stronger.

Don't be afraid of failing. Be afraid of not trying.

While tribulation is universal, how we deal with it is individual. While we fight adversity together, it is our individual effort that will determine the outcome.

To climb a mountain requires us to ascend. The higher and more challenging the mountain, the more difficult will be the ascent.

Too many of us choose less difficult levels. But to reach the top, or to get the most out of life, requires us to accept steep paths.

Don't seek level ground in life. Push yourself to climb higher and harder and reach the top of that mountain called success.

It is within your reach if you have the will to press on and not give up.

The power of concentration is the ability to focus our efforts to accomplish the task at hand.

It is a power like no other. People with this power get more done because they don't let themselves get distracted.

The power of concentration takes real discipline and practice. If you want to get more done, develop this unique power of concentration. You must learn to shut out the distractions around you, period.

What makes one person more successful than another is "sacrifice".

Sacrifice is the willingness to give up something of real value now for the benefit of something greater in the future: such as an education.

The more we are willing to sacrifice near term to gain something better in the future will go a long way to helping us succeed.

Can anyone learn to do the "Tough Things First"?

The answer is absolutely if you are willing to make it a priority and a habit.

It starts with eating the ugly frog first thing every day until you develop a taste for them, to love the things you hate.

"Never ever stop trying" was my mother's admonition to me while I was growing up. It became a drumbeat in my head that resonated with me throughout my life and still does to this day.

I attribute my success in large part to this.

I learned that there is no such thing as not doing my best. To never stop trying and always doing one's best is the hallmark of success. Here's to never stop trying.

Good is good, best is better, but outstanding should be the goal.

We should never be satisfied with anything other than "outstanding". "Outstanding" is outperforming what is expected. We all have high expectations, so when you exceed expectations, you will be considered "outstanding".

If you always exceed expectations, you will never disappoint. This is where success breeds success. Don't just do your best, be "outstanding".

Hoping  or waiting for things to get better is passive. Digging in and making things better is active.

Be active, not passive.

We enjoy success but not failure.

If failure is the lack of success, then all we have to do is turn failure into success and then we can enjoy it.

How do you spell "success"? W-O-R-K. So, if we want to enjoy success, we need to enjoy  WORK.

I predict that those who are not enjoying success are those who are not enjoying WORK. So, the key to enjoying success is to enjoy WORK.

Some people say that "no one is perfect". This would indicate that we cannot be perfect. But let's take a look at what it means to be perfect.

Perfection is the condition state or quality of being as free as possible from any flaws or defects. I say, that based on this definition, we all can be perfect if we are willing and able to rid ourselves, as much as possible, from any defects.

The argument against this is that as humans, we do not have the nature or willingness to rid ourselves of all flaws or defects. It is just too much work! It is this very argument that prompted me to write my book, "Tough Things First". If you are willing to do the tough things first and loving the things you hate, you can get closer to perfection. It takes sacrifice and a burning desire to become perfect.

No matter how many times you are told or believe can never be perfect, stop and rethink what it means to be perfect. Take stock of where you are not perfect and begin, one by one, to rid yourself of that defect or flaw. Once you start on this course, you will see that through persistent effort, you too can become perfect.

Ideas are a dime a dozen. To make an idea worth millions takes ingenuity, creativity, and determination.

There is a saying, "to suffer death by a 1000 bee stings". I believe the saying should be, "life can be bolstered by 1000 bee stings".

We know that children, who suffer from a peanut allergy, can develop immunity to peanuts if given small doses of peanuts over extended periods of time. In the same way, we can develop immunity to difficult challenges if we embrace them and learn from them.

Bolster your life by thriving when dealing with difficult daily challenges.

The "motion of commotion" is always with us and will be so as long as we live.

Most of us will endure a calamity of pandemic proportion every 10-15 years. It is just the nature of mortality. Wish as we want, we cannot change this. We can only endure it.

How we endure it is a personal test of our character and resiliency. It takes courage and fortitude to come out the other side stronger and better.

If you avoid tackling one challenge, you'll likely avoid tackling challenges all together.

Tackling a challenge is like exercising, it takes effort and discipline. If you learn to do the Tough Things First, you will take on challenges and love to do so.

Smaller is bigger when it comes to making changes. It is like eating an elephant. Rather than swallowing the whole elephant in one bite, take smaller bites until the elephant is consumed.

Making small changes and repeating them often will have a bigger impact than making big changes that do not stick. Try this technique as you think about improvements you want to make this next year.

A diamond is the hardest substance on earth. Its brilliance and value come from its hardness.

Pound for pound the diamond is the most valuable substance in existence. The formation of a diamond is created through great pressures and time.

It is similar for us. It is through great pressures and time that we become more valuable. It is the process of hardening that we can endure the test of time. To increase your value, welcome life's pressures and endure to the end.

Dream big or stay unfulfilled. It is your choice!

Most of us do not measure up to our full potential because we just don't dream big enough. Having that vision of greatness is crucial to being what we truly can become.

Don't let your greatness go to waste, dream big.

Life is not easy, but the challenge is to make it worthwhile. You can do this if you have the right attitude and motivation.

You don't have to be rich or even try to be rich to make life worthwhile. To make life worthwhile you need to set some meaningful goals that are important to you and then work like heck to meet them. It's not setting the goals that's the challenge it's working toward them.

To make this happen, set some baby step goals that you know you can achieve and then increasing the goals as you accomplish them. Remember life is not a sprint it's a marathon. Learning to set goals and accomplishing them is the key. Your life is like a puzzle, but all the pieces have to come together to paint the beautiful picture that is worthwhile.

It's all about learning to set goals and accomplishing them.

Making mistakes is not failing but rather a process of learning.

Thomas Edison once said (paraphrased) that when he invented the light bulb that "it wasn't a result of 1000 mistakes but rather the result of a 1000 steps of learning". When we learn from our mistakes we grow in learning, knowledge, and wisdom. Our mistakes are failures when we fail to learn from our mistakes.

There is a saying that I have which is "those who repeat the past, fail in the future". Don't be afraid of making mistakes but do be afraid of not learning from mistakes.

Life's challenges can come in small or large doses. All challenges that beset us, that are not of our own doing, can work for our good and benefit, if we face them with the right attitude.

Don't let a good challenge go to waste: learn and grow from it.

Is the world your oyster?

This is in reference to the pearl created by the oyster. The "pearl" is created by a piece of sand irritating the oyster.

Just like the oyster, you need to take the irritations and create something of value. So, when you get irritated think of the oyster and create something good from it.

Just like the best things in life are never free, it must hold then that the worst things in life must be free.

But how are the worst things in life free? Because they require little or no real effort. Hard work  brings us joy and satisfaction. It is called "a good day's work".

Get the best out of life: work, work, work.

Fear is the author of defeat.

US President Franklin D. Roosevelt said, during the dark days of WWII, "We have nothing to fear except fear itself".

We cannot overcome the challenges we face if we are fearful. It takes unrelenting courage to meet our everyday challenges. This means we must defeat the urge to be fearful. We must stamp fear out of our lives as though it were a dreadful plague.

We can do this if we have hope.

Hope gives us the courage to manhandle fear. In the famous painting by George Fredrick Watts, "Hope" is depicted a lady in threadbare clothing, sitting on a globe, playing a harp with only one string. The lady appears destitute but not hopeless as she tries to get music from the single string.

No matter how down and out you may be, as long as you have but one string left to pluck, you have hope. Don't give up. Erase any fear or doubt you have, and you will succeed.

Diligence is the consistent pursuit of excellence. "Ruthless" diligence is the unwavering, dogged pursuit of excellence in everything good that we do.

We are vigilant as we always do the "tough things first".  We never procrastinate doing those things that enhance our chances to succeed.  We become relentless in doing our very best. It is not enough to try to do our best. We must do our best.

Be "ruthless" in your efforts to succeed and succeed you will.

To "take it on the chin" means you can "take a lick'n and keep on tick'n".

It is the solid, well founded person that can take life's challenges and come out on top.

Be that kind of person and you will never be defeated.

Surviving is just hanging on.

Thriving is just the opposite of surviving. Thriving is getting the most out of life.

During difficult times it seems that all we can do is just hang on. It takes creativity and ingenuity to thrive during hard times.

So, during trying times, just don't just hang in there, beat the odds and thrive.

Do you have the "right" stuff refers to the kind of moxie it takes to be a winner?

A winner is someone who has the intestinal fortitude to surmount all the many challenges and obstacles they will face to be a winner. Winning is like running a marathon: you will hit that wall, when your body says, "I'm done" and screams for you to stop.

Make no mistake about it, if you strive for success, you will hit those walls. Breaking through is the key to being a winner in life. Whether it is beating cancer,  getting an education, a better paying career, marriage or financial problems, or whatever other issue is sapping your strength, when your body or mind says, "I'm done", you must press forward with an eye singularly focused on winning.

To work is a blessing, not a drudgery. Providing for oneself and family is what life is all about. Letting others take on this role, when we are perfectly capable, is not accepting responsibility for our life and family.

Be responsible; work with a vengeance.

Triumph over adversity by meeting the challenge head-on.

You do this by not succoring to adversity but rather looking at the challenge as an opportunity to grow.

Climbing up a mountain is much more challenging than going down. It requires much more energy, persistence, desire, and confidence.

Climbing the mountain of success is no different. During the climb we face all sorts of obstacles that, at first, look like barriers. We can become discouraged, tired, and maybe even injured. For those who can endure the climb of the mountain to success will find that exhilarating feeling of accomplishment. The climb is worth it for all those that can endure.

Be that enduring person and reap the rewards of one who can persevere.

If you don't do your best in any endeavor, a bad habit will ensue.

"Any task worth doing is worth doing well". I might add, "any task you do is worth doing well". This ensures you will develop the right work ethic.

I recently read where a woman survived almost three weeks while being lost in the jungles of Hawaii.

When asked how she managed to survive she replied, "I never gave up hope".

Her answer is the same for all survivors. They just never give up hope.

Motivation is the reason we act in a particular way.

Thus, to be well motivated we need a "good" reason. There are always good reasons to do things, but we tend to minimize or procrastinate acting upon those good reasons.

This is why I preach doing the Tough Things First. Once we develop the habit of doing the truly tough things before the other ones, it becomes much easier to act upon those good reasons and thus our true motivations.

Stay motivated by doing the Tough Things First.

American pioneers met tremendous obstacles as they crossed the plains and mountains of the West; they had no roads, they had few trails, and they had only crude equipment to bring their entire families over rough terrain.

Entrepreneurs are the modern equivalent of those pioneers. Like those intrepid adventurers, entrepreneurs are seeking a better life. Americans don't quit when there are obstacles or challenges. Same with every true entrepreneur, we simply don't give up.

"There is no end in sight."

We say this when our troubles never seem to have an end. But just like the storms that occur every spring, these troubles that seem to be endless do come to an end at some point.

If you are facing what seems to be an endless stream of challenges, know this, "these things too shall pass".

Are you a survivor?

If so, then you are positive and optimistic. You make the bitter better. You make lemonade out of lemons. You turn darkness into light. You brighten the lives of others. You cheer up the sad and make them feel glad. You are caring and determined. You focus on the good in others. You fill them with hope, not despair. You are loved because you bring out the best in yourself and others.

You do the Tough Things First.

They say, "you can't win them all". This is a defeatist attitude and a saying we only use when we get beaten. I say, "you can win them all" if you have the right attitude.

"Winning" is a matter of perception. If we do our best and even if the outcome of the event did not go in our favor, our perception should be that of a "winner". "Winning" is all about doing your very best. Not necessarily having the outcome be in your favor.

When clouds of adversity dim our hope, all we can do is hang on.

Like the storm clouds that bring us weather, there is always a brighter day that follows. Adversity, just like storm clouds, have value.  It makes us appreciate life all the more when the bad times pass. Just like the rain that brings us much needed moisture, adversity brings perspective and points out the areas where we need to grow.

Don't be averse to adversity. We grow through overcoming the vicissitudes of mortality.

Being disabled doesn't mean you are handicapped. A "handicap" is too often a crutch to get others to feel sorry for you.

The road to recovery can be a very long journey. Not finishing that journey assures you will not see the benefits of all your efforts.

Take the challenge and finish the journey no matter how difficult the trip may be.

"No guts, no glory" implies that it takes intestinal fortitude to succeed in business.

Never give up, never.

We all face hills that appear too big to climb. These are unfortunate obstacles that beset us but hope and pray never do.

This is why we hope for the best yet expect the worst.

The conundrum is that we really don't expect the worst will ever happen to us, so we are not prepared for it when it does. Thus, the proverbial saying is an oxymoron. Hoping for the best but not expecting the worst is unrealistic and leaves us vulnerable.

Does this mean that we shouldn't be hopeful and just assume the worst? I don't believe so, because we would all become pessimists, who live miserable lives. They are not happy people. Instead, be optimistic. You will live a happier and more fulfilling life. When terrible obstacles happen to us – and they will – just smile and be of good cheer knowing that these bad times will ultimately pass.

We all want to be better people. The only thing standing in our way is ourselves.

Being a better person requires a little discipline. However, disciplining ourselves can be difficult. Being disciplined takes courage, fortitude and commitment because you are trying to overcome the "natural man", your base desires.

The "natural man" is greedy and selfish. "I want what I want when I want it." Things like anger, lust, lying, cheating, deceiving, teasing, and boasting are related to being a "natural man". Overcoming these selfish attributes takes discipline.

Since thought usually precedes action, undisciplined thought leads to low levels of self-discipline. You have to develop habits to force undisciplined thinking from your mind. Singing a song, biting your tongue, slapping your wrist ... whatever it takes to reprogram your discipline.

Make this your resolution: fight your natural man.

The more you do the more you can do. Don't waste your life, it's the only one you have.

When you have two or more equal priorities to address, do not panic or get distressed. Take a deep breath and set about dealing with them. You might consider flipping a coin to decide which priority to tackle first. In this way it may take a little of the stress off the decision and you can blame it on the coin toss.

Change is what you need to do in order to improve. Increase your rate of change and you will have more change in your pockets.

Want to be wildly successful? Learn to do the *Tough Things First*. Otherwise, procrastination becomes the by-word and failure will be just around the corner.

The more we wish for, the more time we waste. Wishing is nothing more than hopeful thinking. Hoping is like flipping a coin: it is purely statistical.

To make your dreams come true takes sacrifice and above all a lot of blood, sweat and tears. Don't waste your time hoping things will go your way: make it happen. The harder you work, the luckier you get.

Rise up, there is little you can't do if you put your heart and mind to it. We are all far more capable than we think. No matter what your state in life is, you are here on earth for a reason. Find that reason and develop it.

"I can't win for losing," sighed a friend recently.

We all have days like this when we feel as if the world is against us.  Taking a deep breath and saying to yourself, "these things too shall pass" will help you get on with it.

There is indeed "always tomorrow" as the song from the play "Little Orphan Annie" claims. Just grin and bear it when the going gets tough, then get going.

I have discovered an important principle. People who can't seem to make up their minds are by nature just plain lazy. To make a decision of any importance takes a lot of work. When someone says, "I just can't decide", what they are really saying is, "making a decision is too much work".

They either want someone to decide for them or they just postpone making the decision. If you don't make the decision yourself, ultimately it will be decided for you. Don't be lazy, take control of your life and do the necessary work to come to the right decision.

Move quickly or die slowly.

Survival depends on moving quickly when issues arise. Ask anyone who has been attacked by a lion. Not taking quick action is also the reason so many companies fail within the first three years.

Too many startups mistakenly believe that their situation is better than it really is. Instead, all companies and especially startups should operate under the assumption that you will die tomorrow.

Take action today and you are more likely to survive. Do it today or die tomorrow.

If a human heart stops beating, it may require a massive jolt of electricity to restart it.

As the CEO or leader of your company or organization, you are the heart of that organization. When you cease energizing your organization, you need to be re-energized. Otherwise, the corporate body will fade and fail.

Re-energizing yourself takes careful reflection on the reasons you lost your mojo. To get this back requires more effort than you think.

Of course, it is best not to lose your mojo in the first place. A heart requires much less energy to keep it beating ... until it stops. Once it stops, a huge amount of energy is required to get it beating again.

But if you do lose your drive, get back on track with a
vengeance. Half steps won't be enough.

Winning has two major components: passion and persistence.

Passion is a deep, burning love and clear vision for the
venture.

Persistence is that "dogged" drive to stick with the venture no
matter what challenges you face.

Master passion with unrelenting persistence and you can be a
winner.

Determination has the quality of being "unstoppable", which
explains why it is at the core of the culture of the American
military.

You acquire the quality of being "unstoppable" by having an
optimistic "can do" attitude. You seek reasons why it can be
done, not why it is difficult to do. And you try, and try, and
try again until you succeed.

Start by eliminating the word "can't" from your vocabulary.

Remember, determination comes from the heart, not the mind.
It is deeply rooted in our character and nature. It is up to you
to build this important quality – no one else can do it  for you.

All winners are born losers.

Everyone starts off in life at the same point; having not accomplished anything. It takes time and perseverance to become a winner. It doesn't matter whether you are rich or poor, good looking or ugly, well-educated or uneducated. How tenacious you are in pursuing success determines your success.

Success is simply overcoming failure. There is but one course to follow on the path to success, and that is to try. If you do not try, much less try to succeed, you will fail.

How hard you try to succeed is determined by the level of effort you put into it. Winning follows a natural law of physics. Winning is directly proportional to effort.

Human nature causes people to offer excuses when they are not succeeding. This is a dangerous habit. Excusing failure only results in more failure.

Success begins by never providing ourselves with an excuse for not succeeding. Instead, believe in the axiom, "stick to the task until it sticks to you". There is no such a thing as, "I can't". Change it to "I will".

After all, "when there is a will, there is a way".

I realize that this appears Pollyannaish, but is it? This goes to another saying, "making lemonade out of lemons". Most of us get a little too comfortable and lazy about our employment. Just remember, it was when you were out of a job or looking for a new job that you found this one.

Just look at this reduction-in-force a a chance to step up and get a better job. Losing your job may be in fact a real blessing. Who wants to work for a company that doesn't value your work or feels it is important? Just smile and move on.

To be obedient, to comply, or to conform – they all sound the same but are they really?

To comply or conform doesn't require doing so willingly. But obedience does. Love factors into being obedient. We are so because we believe it is the right thing to do.
Nothing, I say nothing trumps experience. No amount of higher education can ever overcome a lack of experience. All research is tied to experience. In other words, all knowledge is experienced based.

We gain knowledge through trial and error. There is a belief that we learn more through failure than through success. This is "bass ackwards".  You only achieve success by overcoming failure. True failure is the direct result of not finding a solution. You show me a successful person and I will show you a person who persists and never gives up until they find the right solution. Experience wins every time.

The pursuit of "easy" is the hallmark of "lazy".

There is no trial in "easy" to help us grow. We only grow when we are sufficiently challenged.

There is a saying I often use; "no pain, no gain". We should push ourselves even beyond what we think we can do.

Remember, "Adversity is like manure, it stinks but it helps us grow".

I was watching a TV series called "Undercover Billionaire". One of the contestants offered three things you must do to be successful.

1. You must be a super salesman.
2. Always be on time for any business appointment.
3. Never give up even when you are discouraged.

"It's not what we have been through but how we have come through that matters."

Scaling a treacherous mountain is not the problem, it is overcoming our fear of falling or failing that gives us anxiety. It is not the climb we fear but the lack of courage to continue that prevents us from succeeding.

Fear is that enemy to success. Overcoming that fear is the key to success. If we continue, without fear, to climb those seemingly endless treacherous mountains of life's challenges, we will reach the summit and raise our arms in that symbolic gesture, "I did it!"

# Relationships

Are you tolerant? Take this simple test to find out.

Ask yourself if you think ill of others who don't agree with you. If you say "no", then you are tolerant.

When it comes to judging someone's actions or statements, do you at first give them the benefit of the doubt or just jump to a conclusion?

To give someone the benefit of a doubt before jumping to a conclusion, means that you get your facts straight before you come to a conclusion. This is hard to do when our minds are already made up.

To train ourselves to be sure of our facts before jumping to a conclusion means that we have to favor love and mercy over judging. Mercy can only trump judging when we are a truly loving person.

Loving our fellow man has to be one of the key motivating factors when it comes to judging our fellow man no matter who they are.

A physician's role is to heal the sick, not to judge them.

We should be like a physician. We should help people to heal and not judge them even if their illness or mistake is of their own doing.

Soar with eagles or flop around with ducks.

This statement refers to how we live our lives and who we associate with. The kinds of people you associate with, has in part, a big influence on your life. Being around and associating with successful people will help motivate you to be successful.

Driving home your point requires hitting the nail on the head.

Most of us do glancing blows and end up not making our point. To avoid glancing blows you must keep your eye on the nail as you swing the hammer. In other words, know your "point" well before you make it.

Being gracious is an attribute that seems to be lost these days.

Graciousness disappears when we focus on what we want and need, and this is a byproduct of selfishness. Anger and frustration results.

Pushing aside your own is being gracious. Let graciousness reign in your life and make life pleasant for others.

We all have a sphere of influence: a significant impact on others.

What is your sphere? It is bigger than most of us realize. Just look around you. Everyone you see every day is within your sphere and you have some impact on them whether it be for good or for evil.

Be an influence for good for all those within your sphere.

Don't just sit around and stew when things are not going right. Grab on to something that will cheer you up.

When you are cheerful, you will bring happiness and joy to all those around you.

Making a life for yourself begins with a knowledge that there will be ups and downs.

Preparing for the ups is not as crucial  as preparing for the downs. It is the downs of mortality that can cause us more pain and suffering.

As with the current pandemic, we should not fear the downs but rather be prepared. Like wearing face masks are to minimize the chances of passing or catching the virus, we should acknowledge that the downs in life can be catastrophic.

Just like taking precautions to avoid illnesses when we are healthy, we need to foster our relationship with others during good times so that during the bad times, those strong relationships will benefit us like having a healthy body.

Often when we are upset with someone we will retort with "what's your problem?"

This makes the situation tenuous at best. Rather than deepening the problem, smile and say, "how can I help you?"

True love is going through a tragedy with a friend.

We can deal with almost anything with a friend at our side. This makes friends so important since we all face challenges so frequently.

God bless our friends.

Kindness is like a bank account, the kinder we are the more we add to our bank account.

A kindness bank account is far more valuable than money. It costs us nothing yet bears tremendous interest.

Money does not always bring happiness, but kindness does.

Who can you really trust? Think about this.

There is a story told about a mountain hiker who was coming back down the mountain and found this poisonous snake shivering in the cold. The snake begged the mountain hiker to take him down the mountain with him to warmer temperatures.

The mountain climber said, "oh no, you'll bite me". The poisonous snake said, "I promise you I will not bite you if you'll take me down the mountain". The hiker felt sorry for the snake and agreed. The hiker then placed the poisonous snake inside his warm jacket and took the snake down the mountain. Once they reached warmer temperatures, the hiker removed the snake and the snake immediately bit him.

The hiker exclaimed with alarm, "you promised that if I brought you down the mountain you wouldn't bite me". The snake immediately retorted, "you knew what I was when you picked me up".

I like this analogy, "holding a grudge is like drinking poison and expecting the other person to die".

Grudges serve no purpose other than to canker our lives, cause us to lose focus, disrupt relationships, and make us less productive.  When you feel a grudge or a resentment developing, shake it off immediately before it kills you.

When you greet someone, just assume they have some significant challenge in their life, and you will be right more than 50% of the time.

Treat them with compassion and empathy. It will go a long way to helping them deal with the adversity they face. The byproduct will be that they are more likely to reciprocate by treating others in the same way.

Why do people argue? Often because they do not have the facts.

When the facts are clear and indisputable, there is no argument or dispute. The more people debate their position, the less substance they have behind their position.

Opinions are nothing more then disputable facts. Avoid an argument, stick with the real facts.

An argument is a contest where there are no clear winners, only losers. Hard feelings inevitably result. Avoid hard feelings anytime you can.

There are just some people who are miserable and want others to feel the same.

You can recognize these types because they are so critical of others.

People who are well-adjusted and have a good self-worth, need not be critical but rather are helpful and up-lifting.

Whose side are you on?

It seems like we are all expected to take sides.  Why is this?

If we are to get along, we must be careful about taking sides. While it is natural for us to take a position, it will lead to discord.

Keeping one's position to oneself it is not always easy, but it certainly will help you avoid unwanted arguments.

When someone says something that offends you, don't overreact. Either just walk away or give them the benefit of the doubt.

If you want to be happy and enjoy life, don't let others ruin it. You are the only one that controls how you feel.

The term, "fighting fire with fire" is when we use extreme measures to attack a problem.

The unfortunate thing is this too often makes matters worse.

For example, if we lash out at someone and the other person lashes back, it may appear as "fighting fire with fire" but this is not only extreme it usually  makes matters much worse. Now the battle is on. Responding with a sulfurous outburst to retaliate may make you feel better because you feel inclined to defend yourself. However, this just causes the battle to rage on and dire consequences can result.

How to handle this rather than "fighting fire with fire"?

Be the better person. Put your flamethrower away. Just move on and not engage in the rampage. It will soon blow over and when calmer minds prevail, you might find a better climate to discuss the issue. It has been my experience that these battles are not worth the fight anyway. Try smiling and "turn the other cheek".

Holding on to intolerant opinions is like fastening a safety rope to a rotted tree. It most likely will not hold you safely and will only give you a false sense of security.

Keep such opinions to yourself and, more importantly, don't let them affect your behavior.

"I'm right and you're wrong and I don't care what evidence you have to the contrary."

This is just being stubborn. Stubborn has its roots in "pride". We all know that "pride" precedes the fall.

Recognizing that we are being stubborn is one of the most difficult characteristics to change because  we are stubborn. The key to minimize the propensity to being "stubborn" is to control our "pride".

It is our pride that dramatically influences our relationship with others. When we seek to denigrate other people who don't agree with our position, it is harmful and destructive.

To change this destructive behavior, we need to suck in our pride and allow others to have their view and opinions. In a word it is humility that allows us to fight stubbornness. Be humble and help us fight divisiveness.

Holding a grudge is like holding a hand grenade in your hand with the pin pulled. It could ultimately kill you. Don't hold grudges and live longer.

Our fundamental relationships remain intact. So why then do we differ? Why is there so much polarization?

It just might be our biases. Our views are not aligned. We just choose to agree to disagree. This in and of itself is not necessarily bad.

What is bad is that we don't just leave it there. We take it to another level and thus become "disagreeable", antagonistic even.

This is where the conundrum lies. Being able to disagree without getting angry.

We need to be tolerant in our disagreements. This is where true respect plays a part. When you feel your anger build, just bite your tongue, count to 10 or whatever it takes. We must learn to accept that we differ and move on without blowing our stack.

It is always easier to say you are sorry before you make the mistake. Therefore, either say you are sorry before committing the error or avoid the mistake in the first place.

"To err is human, to forgive is divine."

It is our nature to make mistakes. Yet too often we do expect everyone to be perfect. "You can't make a mistake if it affects me!" Yes, just admit it. You don't allow others to make mistakes that impact you.

This is why we hold grudges, and thus where we need to change our hearts: forgiveness is the divine nature we need to adopt.

Stop calling the kettle black. After you quit making mistakes, then you can hold your grudge. In the meantime, be forgiving and let go.

When we go shopping for clothes, we look for the clothing that fit our bodies, style and taste. We don't go around expressing vitriolic and slanderous feelings of contempt for the clothing that does not fit our size, style or taste.

Yet we readily do this regarding those with whom we disagree. This makes no sense, but it has become the paradigm of our society today.

No one should care or know how you feel about a particular person or persons if your feelings are vitriolic and condemning.

The way you treat your family is the way you will treat others even if you disagree with this.

This is our nature, and we don't change just because we leave home.

You need not ask your associates what kind of a person you are, just ask your family.

If you practice saying "thank you" for three weeks, it will become a habit. If you develop this valuable habit, it will serve you well in business and at home.

When you encounter a person doing something with which you don't agree, and you would like to have a good relationship with them, you will need to change your view. As they say, "you can attract more bees with honey than you can with vinegar".

This is not to say you have to agree with them. Just don't stop loving them.

To love them means you have to accept them irrespective of their faults. None of us are perfect and we do and say things which are not pleasing to everyone, but we still want to be loved and not judged or condemned. While this is not easy, because we may be seriously hurt and abused, it is none-the-less our duty to change our view and forgive.

To forgive and forget is to love unconditionally. It is not easy, but it is God's way.

It is never too late to say I'm sorry. It is only too late to never take action on a problem. Problems most often do not resolve themselves. They only get worse if not dealt with quickly.

When there are no consequences, people will do stupid things.

It is hard to be friendly when you are in a bad mood.

Here is a tip to turn your moodiness into creating a great day. Smile for one straight minute. It works like magic!

None of us are perfect. Consequently, we all have either hurt someone or have been hurt by others.

This situation can weigh heavily upon us until it is resolved. It can ruin our lives and the lives of those around us. It will not go away on its own.

This is where your hour of reconciliation can resolve cancerous situations.

It takes courage and love, but it can be done by everyone. Don't let the burden of grudges weigh you down. Resolve them immediately. They will only get worse over time.

Be loyal to family, friends, and country. Never criticize anyone before looking at your own weaknesses.

Fighting back is the inability to reconcile differences. Be a reconciler, not a fighter.

When life seems dark and dreary, it is primarily that you are focused on yourself. You never know how good you have it until you reach out to help another having it worse than you. Even just a smile or a friendly "hello" will brighten their day and yours.

If you are easily offended, maybe you are a little too proud.

Put others on a pedestal and you will never become offended.

Hatred is born in the heart. When there is enmity toward another person, you develop a cancer that can only be cured when you remove those angry feelings that are buried deep within your soul. You can never be truly happy when you harbor bad feelings toward another.

Most political leaders are concerned about their "approval rating". I think this is a misnomer.

An "approval rating" is what percentage of those polled like what you are doing. Since the polls don't reveal what they like and don't like about how you are doing your job, this "approval rating" is more about how they "like" you as a person.

Now to my point. Think back when you are doing performance reviews or receiving a performance review. If you are "liked" personally by your supervisor, you are more likely to get a good review and the same if you are the supervisor reviewing one of your subordinates.

The key is being well liked both within the organization and without. Unfortunately, it is not so much how well you are doing your job but more to do with how well you get along.

There is a saying, "what goes around, comes around". Remembering this, we need to be careful how we judge others.

While it is best never to judge, if we do find ourselves judging, judge fairly as we would like ourselves to be judged.

No good compromise can be achieved without friendly persuasion.

There is a biblical saying, "Don't cast your pearls before swine". It basically means, don't waste your time debating with someone who does not share your values or beliefs. So then, why do we do this anyway?

The short answer is simply we just like to argue, or we begrudgingly think we can change their mind. It is very unlikely we will change their mind so all we are going to accomplish is getting angry and upset.

To be truthful, you must not only be clear about what you are saying but also say it in a timely manner. Because "the truth sometimes hurts" we are often reluctant to be totally upfront and transparent with our message. We get caught up with the desire to be tactful.

However, being tactful often dilutes the truth.

Be sensitive about how and where you are being brutally honest. Your delivery of the truth should be in private so as not to embarrass. Be kind and loving when delivering a tough message. If the person agrees with you then there will be no hard feelings. If, on the other hand, they do not agree, they will become very defensive.

When the other party becomes defensive, it is best not to belabor the point. It will only cause them to become more truculent. Most honest people will reflect on your message and will ultimately admit the truth and deal with it. This is good because a willingness to accept the truth is a sign of an honest person.

Giving regular, honest praise is the surest way of expressing appreciation.

A true friend beats a well-connected acquaintance any day. True friends are hard to find and so are to be treasured.

Grumpy, one of the Seven Dwarfs in the story of Snow White, was always in a bad mood. Nobody liked to be around him except Snow White, who was always trying to cheer him up.

We are all exposed to Grumpys. It is unfortunate that grumpy people are difficult to please, just like in the fairy tale. But are we like Snow White? Do we attempt to cheer them, or do we try to avoid them?

When it comes to dealing with grumpy people, don't encourage them. Don't fight fire with fire. Be as one of the other Dwarfs, Happy.

"Screw me once, shame on you. Screw me twice, shame on me."

We all need to give everyone the benefit of the doubt at first until we find they can't be trusted.

 "He or she that repeats the past, fails in the future." Learn from your mistakes and don't repeat them!

Fights start when one or more people get defensive. This is as true as the sky is blue.

Acting defensively is an act of protection, a move like when you "put up your dukes". You are in effect saying, "those are fighting words".

If you want to avoid an argument, do not react in any negative way to comments or actions that you find offensive. "Let it run off like water over a duck's back".

Stop an argument or fight by not fighting back. Be the bigger person.

A kindhearted person is a rarity these days. But you will know them when you meet one because they are:

- Slow to anger
- Willing to help
- Always courteous
- Willing to speak kindly of everyone
- Polite, never using foul or harsh language
- Charitable
- Generally happy
- Tolerant
- Understanding

There are many other wonderful characteristics of kindhearted people and we need more of them, especially in the political arena.

You can help this by being kindhearted yourself.

You don't know who your friends are until you have a problem."

This saying is so unfortunately true. True friends are there whenever you need them, good times or bad, rain or shine. They don't just show up for social events. And great friends anticipate your needs and are there to fill them.

In today's "me too" society, we need more true friends. Go out of your way to help another even if they are not.

Smiling is the best form of compromise. A nice warm smile does wonders in a difficult situation.

Being a "good" listener is a learnable skill. Here are some suggestions to help develop this "good" listening habit.

- Don't rush the conversation. Give the other person a chance to gather their thoughts. Not everyone thinks at the same speed. Just because they haven't reacted doesn't necessarily mean they are ignoring you.

- Once they do comment, carefully ask a question if you need clarifications.

- Listen with an open mind and heart. Show interest in what their comments are.

- Repeat back what you believe you heard and understood from their comments.

- Remember the power of "Yes". Find ways to agree with them even if you don't necessarily agree. Keeping the discussion positive will result in better communication and understanding.

- Check your state of mind. If you are upset or angry, the discussion will not go well. There may be times when you feel the need to unleash your fury and give someone a piece of your mind. Just remember, that when this happens, no "good" listening will occur.

The redemptive power of love is that power to be able to love unconditionally. It is color blind, non-judgmental, sincere, tolerant, truthful, and without guile. While this kind of love, appears to be fading in our society, we can bring it back in all its glory, if we but become more submissive, tolerant, and less selfish.

Go out of your way to being more caring, cheerful, friendly, hopeful, positive, and uplifting. Rise above the common rancor of negativity. Help bring back the redemptive power of love.

How you treat others will be reflected in how you are perceived by others.

If you treat others well, even if you don't get along with them, you will be perceived as a nice person. If you treat others unkindly, you will be perceived as mean-spirited even if you are doing other things well.

Kindness seems to trump many other important attributes. The Christmas Story by Charles Dickens is a good proxy for what I am talking about. The character, Scrooge in the story was obviously a very shrewd and wealthy businessman. However, in the story he is portrayed as a greedy, selfish, and unkind individual.

You may be a very capable person when measured by your success, but it is how you treat others will be the determining factor as to how you will be remembered and revered.

Statistics show that most of us are more concerned about quality and service than price. Most of the reviews customers give about a product or service discuss quality and customer care.

As an employee, you will be judged in your quality and service as it relates to your job. This becomes your reputation. If you want the highest salary and opportunity for promotions, your quality and service will be the deciding factors.

Finding joy and happiness during a crisis is crucial in maintaining a stable home environment.

Spouses working from home and children being homeschooled is putting a real strain on family life. It will take time to readjust but readjusting we must. Here are some suggestions.

- Take the family on frequent walks during the day.
- Separate the family as much as possible in the house.
- Have some special treats over and above the usual that the family can look forward to.
- Organize family activities and games to break up the day.
- Keep the home neat and tidy so it will look appealing. Involve the entire family in this.
- Have the family use headphones to minimize noise level.
- Give awards to children who are more helpful.

- Involve the children in planning and preparing the meals

There are those who are glad, mad, and sad.

If you are mad, you are most likely critical and unhappy. You have a scowl on your face. If you are sad, you play the victim. Your countenance is downturned. You tend to be a pessimist.

If you are glad, you wear a smile on your face. You are an optimist. You tend be happy even when things are not going so well.

The way we are is always a choice. People like to be around those that are optimistic and cheerful and shun those that are not. Help the world be a more cheerful place. Smile and the world smiles with you. Look on the bright side and cheer others up.

What is the most important thing in your life right now: family, friends, spouse, work, health? Whatever it is, make sure it stays important. Things that are important must take priority over everything else and the most important tops them all.

Too often, what we think we say isn't what the listener hears. If we want to be correctly understood, there are a couple of things we need to bear in mind.

1. Are we in a good mood? Listeners will read your mood more than your message. Listeners will respond better to the message if you are in a good mood.
2. Before you spout off your message, think if your message is uplifting. An uplifting message is always better received even if the news being sent is bad or critical. Always find a way to make your message palatable.

Being kind, even when your message is harsh, will most likely go over better and there will likely be no misunderstanding.

Obedient behavior is longer lasting because it is heartfelt. There is respect involved. Individuals comply or conform because of pressure or intimidation. Once that pressure is gone, the need to comply or conform disappears.

To obtain or solicit obedience is more difficult to achieve. It takes a great deal of love and respect from both parties. It must be viewed as a win-win. Otherwise, the need will be perceived as one-sided and the result will be short lived.

Our character is unique to each of us. While we may be similar in some respects, we are all different and this makes us individuals.

We all experience life differently. Our physical makeup/genetics/gender, social environment, culture, education, upbringing, and so many more will define our character. Many of these factors are outside our control and therefore should be considered when judging others' character.

"We should not judge another until we have walked two weeks in their shoes." Therefore, accept the fact that we are all uniquely different and not judge others by our standards.

Hate is one of the most destructive emotions we humans can have toward each other. This abhorrent feeling is what causes so much distress in our society today. Hatred leads to distrust and emotional instability. Hatred blinds us.

When hatred prevails, it is impossible to see the good in others. In fact, it makes us to refuse to acknowledge any good even if it is right before our eyes. We are blinded by the anger and frustration brought on by this vile emotion.

Fighting hatred requires a 180 degree change in our view concerning the purpose of life. The correct view is to become better people, more kind, righteous, tolerant, understanding, caring, considerate, and most of all, more loving.

If you feel any hatred toward anyone or thing, turn around and fight this feeling with all your might, mind and strength.

I have been pondering the word "allegiance", especially as it relates to marriage. With the divorce rate over 50% in the U.S. we need to rethink the meaning of the word "allegiance". Allegiance means to be loyal or committed.

When we get married, we take an oath of allegiance to our spouse. Being loyal or committed means we will not turn away from our marriage partner regardless of temptations or circumstances.

Are there extenuating circumstances that might result in a marriage breakup? Yes, but due to no fault of your own. This then becomes a tricky situation since most breakups have two sides. Seldom is a breakup one sided. A souring of a relationship can usually be found in selfishness. Selfishness is closely related to dishonesty. It is a selfish absorption of one's own carnal desires.

If both parties are truly committed to the marriage and have taken an honest oath of allegiance, the marriage will last. The bond in the marriage is the honest commitment to be loyal to each other regardless...

If difficulties arise, and they will, dig into the issues and resolve them quickly. DO NOT TAKE YOUR RELATIONSHIP FOR GRANTED.

When your expectations are greater than you can do is when being your best is not your best.

This mismatch of expectations generally happens when what is expected of you has an impact on someone else. We see this in politics, sports, work, home, and just about everywhere.

Those around us invariably believe we are not doing our best and can do better. While this may be true in some instances, if we are to get along, we need to cut each other some slack.

Before we become unglued, let's take a look in the mirror and see the real problem; us. None of us are perfect and before our judgment is unrighteous, let's give others the benefit of the doubt and truly accept that they are doing their best even if the result doesn't match our expectations.

# Honesty and Integrity

Walking a straight path through life will save you a ton of sorrow and regrets.

Why is it so hard to always choose to do what is right? It is because always choosing to do what's right is not easy or fun.

Always selecting the right alternative takes a huge amount of discipline and courage. You must make a conscious choice that you will always choose to do what is right. It is not immediately rewarding but it is a discipline that you are developing.

Like any good habit, it takes persistence. But it is one of the most important disciplines we can develop. And when you fail, and you will, don't be discouraged … just keep on trying.

The "spirit" of truth is reality; not a fantasy, as some would suggest. When we are completely honest, the "spirit" of truth becomes our reality and not a figment of our imagination.

Don't create "facts" to suit your imagination or reality. This can destroy you and those around you.

If you tell the truth you won't need a good memory.

You can never do the wrong thing for the right reason although some think they can. Fight to do the right and shun the wrong.

Be honest with yourself. You are the only one who can change your attitude.

Is there a new honesty paradigm?

Some people think honesty is taking a backseat, demoted by situational ethics. For example, telling someone you like their dress when you actually loathe it is not being honest. But do we create confusion by being nice while being dishonest?

Honesty relates to attesting to the validity of certain facts, such as telling the whole truth and nothing but the truth. Facts too often are confused with opinions. Opinions are not facts. Facts are indisputable evidence and not opinions. When you attest to something that is true, it is based on indisputable evidence not your opinion.

Honesty cannot take a backseat to anything, situational or not. Whether it be deceiving or lying, complete honesty is paramount if society is to flourish. Don't be opinion-based, be factual. The presumption of innocence is the rule until the facts, not opinions, are born out.

Being the best is not just doing your best. It speaks to your character; your honesty, your integrity, and the way you treat others.

Avoid the victim mentality. Let's consider the victim mentality list.

- Blame
- Rationalize/Self-justify
- Complain/Murmur
- Make excuses
- Find fault/Get angry
- Minimize/Trivialize
- Make demands
- Cover up
- Doubt/Lose hope
- Flee/Avoid
- Self-pity/Victim
- Abandon
- Indecision
- Deny/Lie
- Procrastinate
- Rebel
- Fear

We have a choice. Give up our agency/be a victim or take control of our life and accept responsibility for our actions.

A "con job" is an act or attempt to convince someone of something that is not entirely true.

While this is bad under any circumstance, the worst con jobs are the ones we do to ourselves. If we can't be honest with ourselves, it is unlikely we will be honest with others.

To thine own self be true. Honesty is the best policy at all times and under any and all circumstances.

Is telling the "truth" always fact based? The answer is "no". Unfortunately, telling the "truth" is often the way the person perceives the "truth" to be. People can vary greatly on the way they perceive the facts to be.

Bias plays a huge role in how facts are perceived. This is why there needs to be multiple witnesses to validate the facts. Otherwise, it becomes a "he said she said".

So how do we get to the "truth" without multiple and very credible witnesses? We can't and won't. This is why there is the saying, "only God knows".  When you find yourself in the situation of needing to discern the facts and what is really the "truth", you just may have to go with your gut. But before you go with your "gut", analyze your bias to determine how much your bias can and is influencing your judgement.

When truth reflects upon our senses, the light of understanding begins to shine. This illumination becomes ever more bright once we seek to know and understand truth.

When you know and then speak the truth, you never have to worry about being misunderstood. You also prosper because truth always wins out over deception. You never have to have a good memory when you speak the truth. Honesty is indeed the best policy.

What you seek, you will find.

Seeking out to help others is good and worthwhile. Likewise, seeking out to harm others, no matter in what way, is damaging and of no value what-so-ever. Seeking for something that is damaging or bad but makes you feel good is not a good reason to do the wrong thing. You cannot cover evil by doing something you feel is  needed or important.

Never seek doing evil no matter how good it makes you feel.

Honesty appears to be in short supply especially when it comes to politics, personal matters, and business. What is real honesty? "Real" honesty is telling the whole truth and nothing but the truth, period.

Somehow, when it comes to politics, personal matters, and in business, telling the "truth" is a facsimile of the truth only to the extent it doesn't cause any damage or harm. This is why there are polygraph machines.

There is a saying I like to use. "When you begin to deceive, a complex web you begin to weave." The "real" truth will come out in the end. Be totally honest, even if it hurts. Honesty ultimately pays off.

How do you know when someone is lying? When their lips are moving and they're not listening.

I'm appalled that speaking the "truth, the whole truth and nothing but the truth" appears to be passé (out the window). This paradigm shift seems to have permeated our society.

What this portends for the future is not good for our society. It promotes the notion that it will be viewed as acceptable to not be totally and completely truthful. The media is being flooded with "fake" news. So-called honorable people corroborate this junk, this fake news, passing it off as truthful.

We need to voice our objection to this nonsense or "Katie bar the door" if we never get back to "telling the truth, the whole truth and nothing but the truth".

If you tell a lie often enough, you will believe it to be true.

The reason is simple. We store information in our brains to remember or reiterate something. Once it is stored many times in our memory, we recall it as true. This evolutionary trait helps us advance when we remember facts and is just human nature. But when it turns lies into "facts", it is harmful.

The best way to avoid this awful habit is to never ever lie. Lying is one of the worst habits you can develop. Be a forever honest person and you will build a great life based on integrity.

To "face the music" is an idiomatic phrase for accepting responsibility for one's actions or misdeeds. A lot of Silicon Valley CEOs have recently been facing orchestras.

It is not uncommon for people to think they can get away with something that is not honorable or honest. It is an odd notion that if you do something wrong and haven't got caught, that what you did can't be deemed dishonest. This leads to the false belief that you cannot be punished unless you get caught.

However, just because you haven't had to "face the music" yet, you still carry the psychological burden of your misdeed. Whether you accept this fact or not, ultimately you will have to pay for your behavior.

Don't be lulled into the belief that you got away with it. Just "face the music" and live a happier life.

Studies show that the more religious you are, the more likely you are to have good ethics. The reason appears to be that religious teachings focus on being an honest person and the belief that if you are a good person, you will inherit a better place in the after-life.

While I believe that all people are inherently good, their training in and outside the home, goes a long way in how they view being ethical. This is why I believe that the environment that our children are subjected to is so important to how they will turnout as adults.

Does an admission of guilt mean you are guilty? Yes, for the crime or issue you have confessed. However, not admitting when you are guilty is even worse. Readily admitting, without being forced to do so, is being honest.

As Judge Judy says, "if you tell the truth, you don't need a good memory".

"Crooked" means to be bent out of shape, not straight. It also means to be dishonest. Whenever we are not being straight with someone, this is being deceitful ... crooked.

Sometimes we withhold certain information. In this case we are deliberately trying to deceive them, and that is just one form of being crooked.

Whenever we try to mislead, for whatever be the motive, we engage in criminal activity. Don't be a criminal. Always be straight with others.

Choose "right" when the choice is placed before you.

In that light, let your conscience be your guide. Our conscience has been developed throughout our life and is usually built upon strong principles and teachings. It is when we don't heed those strong principles and teachings that we get into trouble.

The term, "we know better" is what I mean about not listening to our conscience. We should act according to our conscience and this will keep us out of trouble.

# Community and Society

Where there is hatred there is unhappiness and unrest. Where there is love there is happiness and peace.

The difference between Baby boomers, Generation X'er's, and Millennials is about 25 years each. It is amazing how technology and time changes the view of each generation. If we look at each generation as an era, it becomes clearer why each generation has such differing views.

The Baby boomers were from the war era.

Generation X  were from the peace era.

Millennials are from the technology and globalization era.

Over the past 75 years, the subsequent generations have become more focused on the future of the planet and how globalization will impact their lives. Because of technology, the world has become smaller and more accessible.

To get along better, we need to open our eyes and see each generation in terms of how the other generation views the world. No matter which generation we belong to, we all have one thing in common. We are all part of the same human family and should be looking at this like we are one family.

The more you do something the better at it you become whether it be for good or for evil.  It becomes habit forming.

To be a valued person in society, form good habits, not bad ones.

"Be quick to heal and slow to judge."

In this saying, "healing" refers to making things better. "Judging" on the other hand, refers to criticizing and making things worse.

We need more healers and fewer judges.

Overcoming or counteracting free agency can only be done through force.

The use of force, unless done legally, is a form of terrorism. Even the use of legal force must be done carefully, or it will still be deemed as terrorism. Free agency/ personal freedom is such a powerful thing that wars are fought over it.

We value our freedom so much that we will fight to the death to preserve it. Almost all laws are written to protect freedom.

Fight for your freedom and don't take it for granted.

You cannot debunk a falsehood, only the person who is spreading the falsehood can.

Who am I? What makes me special? What makes me unique?

These are questions I have pondered, and I am sure you have also (and every business should do so as well). We are all unique, special people that have an important role to play out here in mortality.

Shakespeare, in the play McBeth, has a line that goes something like this "We are all actors who strut our lives upon the stage and then we are no more." This sounds like our life is very fatalistic and of little value.

This could not be further from the truth. Our life is extremely important and of immeasurable value. Together and individually, we make up the fabric of mortality. Without our unique, special individuality, there would be no earthly life. I am grateful for every living life, its uniqueness and contributions.

Studies show the more we express our gratitude, the more grateful we become.

This is like any other habit we develop – the more you stick to something, the more the habit will stick to you.

Gratitude is a wonderful habit to develop. I have never met a grateful bad person.

The poignant words of Patrick Henry ring loudly in my ears, "give me liberty or give me death".

We have a choice, liberty or tyranny. Liberty is freedom from compulsion and control. Tyranny is the oppressive rule by governments based on the belief that the government is acting in the best interest of society.

Never, ever is oppression and control in the best interest of society.  Tyranny is the antithesis of liberty. Give me liberty or give me death. Let freedom reign.

The sustainability of a viable society requires a different course than we are currently on.

It requires a view of each member of society as valuable, to be loved and respected even if they are not living or performing in accordance with our standards.

None of us are perfect and we should not expect everyone else to be perfect. What we should expect is for us not to be judgmental.

"Do not judge a person until we have walked a mile in his shoes," is an appropriate adage. We need to change course.

Kindness is a key attribute of being righteous.

Righteousness is at the heart of being honorable and good. It is hard to imagine anyone who is good and not kind. Kindness is the quality of being friendly, generous, and considerate.

In today's hostile environment we can all use a bit more kindness toward our fellow man regardless of whether we agree with them or not.

There is a paradigm shift that is taking place in the world today. This paradigm is where good is called evil and evil is called good.

The argument, of course, is defining what is "good" and what is "evil".  Because we come at this with differing moral beliefs and standards, we need to analyze this in terms of the effects of "good"  versus the effects of "evil".

If something is "good", the long effects will remain positive. In other words, there will be no long-term negative consequences. On the other hand, if something is "evil", the long-term effects will be negative.

Therefore, we can classify "good" and "evil" in terms of their lasting value and consequences.

I am intrigued with those who claim to be "undecided" or "fence sitters".

People who are "undecided" are just individuals who don't want to take a stand but trust me, they have taken a stand, at least in their hearts. I know some of you will not agree with this and that's okay since you will have just proven my point.

It seems to be these days that trashing others is the new paradigm. So why do we have this paradigm shift?

This is because the news media seems to dictate how we should treat others. In the news, you rarely hear anything good being said about anybody.

What is the solution? Don't listen to the news or follow social media? This is one way to avoid falling into this nasty paradigm shift pit if you find yourself agreeing with them.

What we expect in others is really what we expect of ourselves. The problem is that we are our own worst critics.

Could this explain why we are so critical of  others who do not measure up to the expectations we have of ourselves?

We can minimize harsh expectations we have of others if we will only be kinder to ourselves. We all have faults and should not look or dwell on others' faults. If we do this, we will not only be a happier people, but we will get along better with others.

A liar these days means someone who doesn't agree with the facts as you see or interpret them. No one is given the benefit of the doubt.

Being called a liar is a very terrible, demeaning and disconcerting thing. Always avoid calling someone a liar unless you are trying to discredit them and deem them to be your enemy.

I was recently discussing with a friend about the current social unrest we are experiencing. It became clear to me that "social unrest" is a definite and unequivocal consequence of the self-centered nature of mankind.

We came into mortality self-centered, focusing on what we wanted and when we wanted it. This self-centered nature is controlled as we mature and recognize that we are not the only ones that have needs.

This thought caused me to ponder the word "sacrifice". "Sacrifice" makes me think of my parents, teachers, and friends that have helped me grow throughout my life. These wonderful people sacrificed their time and resources to help me along my journey through life.

If we are to minimize the "social unrest" we are currently experiencing, we need to rid ourselves of these immature personal focusing on what we want, when we want it.  To do this, we need to focus on sacrificing our needs and wants for the good of others.

"Unity" is the engine that drives harmony and respect.

What causes the unity engine to stall is the belief that you cannot love and respect those who disagree with you. This is a false and dangerous premise.

Unlike eating something that does not agree with you, a difference in opinion should not cause your body to react since the issue is in your mind. This you can control if you want. It begins with a desire to allow others to have their own opinions even if they differ from yours. This then becomes the unifying aspect of unity.

We all think differently and have different priorities. We need to be willing to accept these differences and move forward with love and respect for all.

Inequality and iniquity have the same root. Both are bad.

Inequality stems from hatred and is bidirectional. There is a tendency with some groups to force equality which is a form of inequality in and of itself. You cannot force anything without hatred raising its ugly head.
We should believe and hold to the premise that all men are created equal. It is this premise at which many scoff. They retort, "how can there be equality unless we are all the same, physically, mentally, financially, and sexually".

This belief is absurd on the very face. Created equally should refer to freedom and liberty and nothing else. This is why freedom and liberty are so important to all mankind. No one should ever be deprived of this God given right regardless of their physical, mental, financial, or sexual differences.

This is equality, period. To believe otherwise is iniquity.

Being tolerant doesn't mean you have to agree, but some people think that if you don't agree you are intolerant.

This, I believe, is the reason there is so much animosity between groups with differing views. Being tolerant is the allowing of differing views and opinions without necessarily agreeing with them. It is also a sign of intelligence.

Too many people find it impossible to tolerate differing views or opinions they disagree with. This is where we have a conundrum. Some people are trying to change the definition of the word "tolerance" to simply mean "if you don't agree wholeheartedly, you are intolerant". It is this redefining of the concept of tolerance that is nonsensical.

One major aspect of hatred is jealousy, which is fostered through greed.

So, what drives greed?

In Mosaic law, it is written, "thou shall not covet". Coveting is that powerful urge to possess something. Thus, greed is nothing more than coveting. Both of these nasty human characteristics are born out of jealousy.

Such jealousy drives hatred. Having enmity toward anyone, regardless of our supposed justification, is just plain wrong. Ask yourself if you have any unkind feelings toward anyone. If so, you may just be jealous.

To be "myopic" is to be nearsighted. Being nearsighted means to see only what is just before our face: not looking long term.

This is the problem with selfishness. Selfish people don't see myopia's impact because they are only seeing what they want and need, and not seeing the impact on others. This is "our instant gratification".

To be "farsighted" is to be wise by looking at our impacts into the future. It is being selfless and not yearning for what we want and need. It is a willingness to sacrifice our instant gratification for the betterment of all. It is a win-win focus.

Let's all focus on being more farsighted.

People often try deception when facts don't work. This is one way to get what you want even if it is dishonest. This is how magicians fool you into believing with your eyes when your mind says, "no way".

We live in a time when deception has become a way of life. We have so much more knowledge readily available at our fingertips it is making it more difficult for others to deceive us. This is a good thing unless we don't or won't check/verify our information sources. Remember, just because the information agrees with your beliefs doesn't necessarily mean it is right. This is where it gets tricky.

Our bias can and will influence our beliefs. We can become our own deceivers if we don't look at all sides of the issues.

Don't be a fool by fooling yourself. Believe only a fraction of what you read and even less of what you see. If all else fails, trust your gut. The truth usually lies somewhere in the middle.

Kindness begets kindness, love begets love, honor begets honor, loyalty begets loyalty and so on.

The same for the opposites, hatred begets hatred, anger begets anger, disloyalty begets disloyalty, etc.

There is a price we pay for each of our actions. Nothing is free and without consequences. Our actions define who and what kind of a person we are. As the saying goes, "actions speak louder than words".  "Sow ye sow , sow also shall ye reap." You can't plant corn and expect to reap wheat.

Plant "goodness" and you will reap "goodness".

"Racism" has become a catch all term for anything having to do with a feeling of dislike for something.

This expansion of the term has caused a great deal of confusion since most of us associate racism with the feeling of hatred, distrust, and enmity toward people of a different race. It is this definition, when used against people of a different ethnic background, that is causing the pushback when used to accuse someone of being racist. To call someone racist requires you to know and understand their mindset.

The only one who really knows and understands one's mindset is the person themselves. Judging another's mindset is equally wrong. There is a saying that I like: "you can only change the  things you can control and should only be concerned about the rest".

We/ you can only change our feelings and behavior. We cannot nor should not change others. First, make sure your "house is clean". Condemning others is like "the pot calling the kettle black". It is this condemning, judgmental mess that is causing all the unrest.

Stop judging others and focus on your own behavior. Set a good example for others to follow.  Be a leader, not a follower.

The biggest difference I see between Millennials and Generation X is the Millennials are more dependent on social media for their advice and outreach than Generation X.

Millennials are less likely to interface directly with older people. This becomes a Catch 22 since their advice and interaction on social media mainly comes from their own generation who lack experience. This is a dangerous situation since we now have the blind leading the blind.

How can we reverse this negative situation with the Millennials? It simply has to come through parental involvement. Parents, sit down with your kids and reverse this trend.

The spirit of contention is the drumbeat of today's society.

Its rancor is ever present. We are filled with its lies and deception. The only purpose it serves is to drive a wedge of hatred between us.

But we need not succumb to this. We have a choice, and that choice is to turn off this rancorous noise. Find joy and happiness in listening only to uplifting things that do not stir us up and further foster this spirit of contention.

When you are provoked or undergoing a difficult challenge, can or will you be kind?

If so, you are considered long-suffering. You have a unique quality of being charitable under any and all circumstances. We need more long-suffering people to help us offset the anger and enmity that exists so prevalently in society today.

Examine your feelings and be more long-suffering. We need more kindness.

It is all about the verbiage.

Sometimes we get all twisted around the axle trying not to understand the other person's point. So how do we "try" to understand the other person's point? This is where we are being respectful of others.

If you have an honest and loving heart, you will most likely be completely respectful of others and give them the benefit of the doubt even if goes counter to your point of view.

When you are honestly respectful of others, you will be less likely to enter into a full-blown argument.

Most of us are more than willing to share our unwanted opinions. This usually happens when we have a differing view.

STOP!

Do not offer your opinion if it might cause some hard feelings. In times of divisiveness as we are experiencing in our world, we need to be much more considerate of other peoples' viewpoints. As much as we might disagree, resist with all the vigor you can muster, giving your retaliatory opinion.

For the sake of bringing us closer back together and with the hope of having less divisiveness,  keep your opinions to yourself unless it is necessary to speak them, and we will all be the better for it.

In the famous 1910 patriotic song, "America the Beautiful", there is a verse that goes, "...who more than self their country loved, and mercy more than life".

Given all the rancor and divisiveness we are currently experiencing in America, we could well recall these words and put them into practice.

Let's truly love our country, showing mercy and respect for others more than ourselves.

"Me thinks you protest too much", a Shakespeare character said.

"Protesting" is a right guaranteed under the 1st Amendment. Having said that, what I like about Shakespeare saying is the inference that we protest too much.

What does it mean to protest too much? When it becomes annoying. People just stop listening or paying attention. When we protest too much, people get turned off and we get the opposite effect of what we are looking for. Just like with anything, too much is just too much.

We have two ears and one mouth and should use them proportionally. If we are going to protest, we need to stop and listen twice as much as we speak out.

No matter how much you want or try, you can't effect change in anyone other than yourself. When we seek to effect change in others, we lose or diminish the real focus of continuous improvement of oneself.

This is what I admire in Asian cultures; they focus on how they can improve the group, at the expense of themselves. This is the concept of the true servant leader. I believe this may account for why the Asians do so well in school. They sincerely want to please others, especially their elders. They don't spend a lot of time criticizing others. Rather they focus on how they can improve to help the group. This is a more selfless approach to life.

If you want to have continuous improvement in your life, "look in the mirror, not around it".

What does pride and greed have in common? They both have "selfish" as a root.

Selfishness is so rooted in the behavior we are seeing, not just among the politicians in the US, but amongst all countries around the world. Selfishness is the animosity and unfair actions that others take against each other in the name of "nationalism" or "protectionism".  It is, "every man for himself". It is sometimes "us against the world".

Protecting oneself is defined as preventing someone from harming you. This is where it gets tricky. What is "harming"? This is where we tend to battle. For example, let's say that I have a fishpond on my property, and I pay to have the pond stocked with fish. It is my pond and my fish. However, there are some that view this as selfish because I do not share this asset openly with the public.  While I can see their point of view, the law does protect me from unwarranted trespass. I am not harming the public or being unlawful by excluding them from using my asset.

Bottomline, this is why we have "laws" to define what is harmful. We should obey the laws of those countries or suffer the consequences. Don't be selfish, be law abiding.

Why do we want to fight rather than help each other? Aren't we all on the same tram with the primary goal of making our Nation better? Why does politics have to be so nasty?

Let's put our differences aside and work more diligently for the good of our great country. If we can, we can make everything so much better for all of us. To do this we will have to be more civil. Rather than argue and be so vitriolic toward each other, let the citizens choose who serves best.

The Bible teaches us to love our enemies: those who spitefully use us. Note that this doesn't mean those who you have aught against.

You should not have enmity toward anyone, friend or foe. This is not easy given the amount of anger and hatred they may show against you. It is our nature to protect ourselves against our enemies. So then, how does one go about "loving" our enemies?

Unless there is a threat of physical harm, do not retaliate. Just let it go.

When hatred abounds, anger reigns supreme.

Controlling anger becomes a must or society deteriorates. The key to controlling anger is to not let it take root. Just let it go.

Do not dwell on that which makes you upset. To do this, just think about something pleasant or sing a tune that makes you feel good.

A "victim mentality" is an acquired personality trait where a person tends to view themselves as a victim when the actual evidence doesn't support this feeling. It is a "woe is me" mentality.

This is peculiar in that the person is looking inward. This is a selfish behavior. The more we focus on ourselves, the less we see what is really going on around us. We develop a cocoon of hostility and bitterness that only further divides us.

We need to break out of this destructive cocoon by focusing on the good in others.

Revenge is a form of hatred.

It is an attempt at evening the score. A sense of "justice". An eye for an eye and a tooth for a tooth. So why should this make us feel good?

The prevailing and intense desire to get even is causing much discord in our society today.  We have become sore losers. Under these conditions there is no compromise, so jealousy and envy rule our behavior. Whatever happened to good sportsmanship?

Can we ever reverse this desire for revenge?  I hope so, because if not, we are doomed to ever having a peaceful society. Let's stop the bickering and animosity before it is too late.  The result could be civil war.

Protagoras said to Socrates, "what is truth to you is truth and what is truth to me is truth".

I think truth is truth to everyone and not specific to each individual. In that light I believe Protagoras must have been referring to "good" instead of "truth".

Truth is truth and not selective based on individuality.

There is no such thing as a free lunch. Don't expect or feel entitled to something you did not work for or at least contribute in some fashion. You are only entitled to freedom and the direct pursuit of happiness. The rest you must work for.

Socialism doesn't work unless everyone is willing to "work" whether they think they can't or not.

I thought name calling was something only children did to each other. However, I see this more and more with adults, especially when it comes to politics.

"Sticks and stones may break my bones, but words will never hurt me," was what my mother would quote whenever I complained about classmates that resorted to name calling.

There is no doubt that name calling is divisive. We should ignore it, even in politics. Let's act like good adults and stop condoning name calling. Let's look for the good in others and not the bad.

Truth is the portraying of the facts as we see or understand them.

"Facts" can and often are different than what others see or understand. For example, a colorblind person will see the colors different than someone who is not. Just because the colorblind person see colors differently doesn't mean they aren't being truthful.

Truth then becomes what is in the eye of the beholder, and we all view facts differently depending on our viewpoint. This is why getting to the truth is so difficult. We all want to believe what we want to believe.

Being "lazy" means being unwilling to work or put forth the requisite effort.

The two key words here are "unwilling" and "requisite". Both words have a judgement attribute associated with them. When we call someone "lazy", we are in effect judging.

It is very difficult to be a fair judge. For what gives us the wisdom and knowledge to judge others. There is a saying, "for so ye judge, so shall ye also be judged". Be known as a fair and kind person and do not judge others no matter how strong your bias or feelings may be.

Minimum-wage laws were instituted when employees were not able to organize into a labor union and the government felt it was necessary to step in and force companies to pay a living wage.

But force is never a good thing. The primary purpose of government is to protect its citizens from harm, both foreign and domestic. The key word is "harm". This should have been limited to physical and criminal dangers, but now it has branched into anything the government deems harmful.

Minimum-wage laws are such an example. Government does not trust companies to do what is right for their employees, thus the government imposes a minimum wage. This is just one more step toward socialism.

It is through minimum-wage laws that caused companies to move operations offshore. Companies will always find ways to compete. Minimum-wage laws only work in those instances where companies will not benefit from offshoring.

As a kid we played a game after eating an apple. When we got down to the core, we would say, "apple core Baltimore, who's your friend". The game was for someone to pick out an enemy, not a friend. You would then try and hit this person with the apple core.

Unfortunately, we seem to be playing this game in politics. Just like in this kid's game, we seem to take joy in splattering our opponents. Even as adults, we seem to revel in being childish. Let's start acting like adults and set better examples for our kids. Is it any wonder why our kids grow up being childish?

If you truly love others, you will not harbor any resentment or unkind feelings toward them. This is called unconditional love.

Tribal bonds are entities for which we have strong loyalties. These could be sports teams, political factions, religion, race, family, hobbies and more. Tribal bonds can be weak or strong, but they all shape our opinions and decisions.

Be aware of your strong tribal instincts and don't let them cause you to have bad behavior.

Reaching out and touching the lives of others for good would certainly help mitigate the harsh reality of today's toxic rhetoric. Be an influencer for peace-stamp out hared.

Two of the nicest words in the English language are love and charity. So why aren't these words more prevalent in the media? The quick answer is they sell. Why does toxic and racy news sell better? The quick answer is that this is where our minds are focused.

We need to get our minds out of the gutter and focus more on what is uplifting and good. If we do, then just maybe the news will focus on this rather than the negative.

The First Amendment to the United States constitution protects many rights, including an individual right of free speech. Limits to free speech include such things as not being allowed to slander another individual.

But note that this is an "individual" right, not group rights. As such, most of the limitations on free speech are designed to protect individuals and do not apply to groups. The law can prevent me from falsely claiming that you are a criminal, but it allows me to say that Congress is.

Yet some people now advocate the elimination of the first amendment because they believe it has become a "group" right. They do not believe a person can express opinions that refer to groups of people.

Unfortunately, opposition politics has shoved everyone into groups, depleting their status as individuals. To some I am no longer Ray Zinn, an honest hardworking father trying to provide for my children, grandchildren, and great grandchildren. Instead, I have been demoted to a "privileged", educated, white male who now can't be trusted. I am discriminated against unless I renounce myself of these labels.

What ever happened to the concept of not discriminating based on race, color, religion, social status, or sex because those things are not important to the quality of a person's character? Judge everyone based on how they live their lives and not on what "group" you attach them to.

Animosity fans the flames of discontent. The more we explore our differences, the more anger can burn within us.

Rather we should explore the areas where we agree. Look for the similarities. Look for the goodness.

Put out these fires of discontent and live happily together.

If we cannot tolerate the differences in others, then we are of mankind's most miserable.

However, if we can see in others the goodness that exists, we will overlook the differences that drive us apart.

John Chambers, ex-CEO of Cisco, once said, "If you aren't being disruptive, you will be disrupted".

I agree! As they say in the college profession, "publish or die". Being disruptive is good only if you are challenging the norm or stodginess. Being complacent or unwilling to keep up with the times is suicide.

Being negatively disruptive – such as in social violence – is not good and just breeds unrest. Innovating or seeking change for the good of mankind is different. There is no violence or unrest.

Fact checking" is the process of validating the authenticity of certain information. We all do this irrespective of how we get the information.

But there are people who in effect say, "don't confuse me with the facts since my mind is made up already".

Unfortunately, we can all fall into this trap with just a smidgeon of bias. We just want to believe that our story is accurate even if it isn't. It is our bias that determines whether or not something is factual.

So how should we treat all information? Hopefully, we will do our own fact checking before accepting new information as authentic. First, we should consider the information source and its bias. Second, we should look at multiple sources to insure we hear as many sides as possible. Third, we should analyze the information and determine, in our own minds, if what we are hearing makes any sense. Fourth, make sure our heart is right and not judgmental.

A soft and kind heart will usually get us to the right answers. This is an important part of being a good and rational fact checker.

When the founding fathers passed the first amendment, "freedom of speech", did it mean that we can say or do things intended to harm or incite others to do harm? The answer is obvious, "no". Yet there are some that have extrapolated this to mean the opposite.

So why are we letting them get away with this? The answer is because the definition of "harm" means to physically injure. Being obnoxious, extremely unpleasant, is not specifically causing physical harm but can cause emotional injury.

There is no "cause" important enough to justify obnoxious behavior. It is a crude and unkind person who resorts to obnoxious behavior to get their point across.

Respect for others has to be taught in the home. The reason some cultures, like the Japanese are more respectful is that respect is not only a national culture it is emphasized and reemphasized in the home.

If we are to ever hope to have a respectful culture in the US, we must each start by setting a respectful example even if those around us don't. Let's all commit, starting today, to be a more respectful people.

Forbearance is a quality this nation needs badly. To have forbearance means that you practice.

- Patience
- Tolerance
- Restraint
- Respectfulness
- Soft demeanor
- Kindness
- Bring slow to anger and quick to forgive
- Bring considerate

Forbearance takes self-control. Developing the qualities and characteristics of forbearance will serve you well and bring much happiness and joy to your life.

When I have written about being kind, gentle, and becoming more meek, some think this to mean I propose not taking a stand for righteous and honorable principles. This could not be further from the truth.

We should always stand for noble principles. What I am suggesting is the better way to take our stands.

Foremost we should seek to understand and respectfully consider where others are coming from BEFORE we take our stand. This helps us to respect others, even if we eventually disagree.

Then, when we do take our stand, let us do so in a respectful, nonviolent manner. We should present our position lovingly and not in an arrogant or hostile way.

Differing" brings out the worst in us. Too many people can't seem to tolerate a point of view other than their own. Why?

Differing opinions and viewpoints have always been with us. It is in our nature. All wars, conflicts, divorce, etc., stem from differing points of view. The problem is that they tend to take on tones of animosity.

To overcome the violence associated with differing requires each of us to change our view of it. We need to adopt a "just let it be" attitude. This will help reverse the typical process of being quick to anger and slow to forgive. Let's focus on controlling our anger by finding the good in others who we may differ with.

We all seem to have people we don't care for much. This is just human nature. As kids, when we didn't like someone, we bullied them, called them names or might even try to physically harm them.

As adults we view this childish behavior as deplorable and even try to punish kids for bullying. Well hold on. I see adults doing the same thing. The news is filled with "adults" who are casting dispersion on those they don't like and even physically assaulting them. Many well-known adults have resorted to hiring bodyguards to protect themselves.

No wonder our kids have resorted to bullying. They are just mimicking the adults. If we expect to have a civil society, we need to stop adult bullying too and set the proper example for our youth.

"Nothing in life worth having is free." This old adage is so true and yet so many feel entitled. They claim that the world owes them a living.

But all entitlements come with a cost. Even those who partake of entitlements pay a price: a loss of pride and self-respect. They become takers rather than producers. With this, they tend to be more critical and upset with the world. Entitlements come with a high price and most often are regretted later on.

The only real entitlement we can expect and enjoy is our freedom. Don't waste it by making bad choices and decisions that can cost you this freedom.

It is a shame that with world trade issues and other things, there is no real sharing, no "tit for tat". This unwillingness to share is all about selfishness. We are not thinking about the other guy. It is all about us; what we want and when we want it.

We offer excuses like, "They are richer or better off than us so they should share more." This excuse is at the heart of the problem. It again goes to selfishness. We covet or believe that sharing is one way. We get more until we have enough or more than enough. We loath anyone having more than us. We are just greedy buggers.

Forget this attitude! If you do, you will be happier and more willing to share.

While the nuclear threat around the world rages, there is an equally dangerous threat we face here at home. This threat is the deepening divide between the "right" and the "left".

This divide has resulted in downright hatred and even violence. Oddly, this chasm was brought about through intolerance. Only by eradicating intolerance can we hope to live in peace.

So, what can we do? We all should know that it takes two to fight. Avoid the fight and you avoid generating your own side of intolerance.

We used to say, "sticks and stones may break my bones, but words will never hurt me". Let's revive this saying and stop reacting to any negative verbiage cast our way. If we do, I promise you this divisiveness will begin to subside.

No one makes us intolerant. This decision is made individually.

Because of all the animosity prevalent in our society today, I began to ponder the cause of this. Was it social media, the news media, the political environment, or something else?

Just like no one can make you mad or sad, it is each one of us, individually, that decides how we are going to react to any given situation. Yet, being human, we all too often like to blame others for our bad choices. Somehow, we feel it lets us off the hook. This falsely amplifies animosity, and then intolerance.

Instead of blaming others for these bad choices, take complete responsibility for your actions. If you do, chances are that you will stop making these bad choices and mend your ways.

Intolerance is totally up to you. You can choose to be friendly or hateful. It is your call.

It is crude to be rude.

Rudeness involves being offensively impolite or ill-mannered. There is no excuse to ever be this way and yet we are constantly being bombarded with rudeness in the media, on the freeway, in our schools, at work, on social media, and even at home.

We have become so numb to rudeness we have begun to accept it as normal and okay. This acceptance of rudeness is dangerous because we run the risk of being rude ourselves. When this happens, this awful condition will only get worse.

We need to stop accepting rudeness. Don't just idly stand by when observing such boorish behavior. Politely tell the offender that you do not appreciate their conduct. If you observe rude behavior in the media, refuse to patronize the offending outlet.

Rudeness is quite literally a disease, that spreads in epidemic modes. Help stamp out this horrible illness. It is a cancer in our society that we need to eliminate.

Anger reigns when tolerance doesn't.

Honesty and integrity are related to one's moral views of right and wrong. Moral views are highly correlated to one's religious faith and upbringing.

The more religious and faith based one's moral views are, the more community and society is enhanced. In addition, people of faith tend to be more service oriented. They reach and help their neighbors more willingly.

 Bottomline, religion does benefit society.

One aspect of the 1st Amendment to the American Constitution protects "freedom of speech". This amendment protects citizens from being interned by the government for voicing their opinions. It was not meant to allow unfettered, slanderous or inciting outbursts or attacks.

Unfortunately, just like other protected rights, things have gotten out of hand. Misunderstanding the 1st Amendment has caused civil disobedience, riots, hateful attacks, desecration of revered national ideals, and an "anything goes" mentality. This crippling notion has struck our nation, all under the belief that such uncivil or illegal behavior is somehow a protected freedom of speech and expression.

Never in their wildest dreams did our founding fathers expect this kind of interpretation to take root. Rules and laws are written such that normal, reasonable people would understand and follow them. It appears that we are faced with unreasonable, self-centered people both inside and outside of government, interpreting these laws to suit their own self-serving and unrighteous agendas.

Reasonable people, who have the greater interest in preserving our real freedoms and protecting our nation from radical destroyers need to take notice and move to shut down this nonsensical overthrow of our country and its laws. Protect your real freedoms or lose them altogether.

I have written before about being kind. Some people have asked me why they should have a burning desire to be kind. In other words, what's in it for me?

The obvious religious answer is, "Do unto others as you would have them do unto you." But I began to wonder if there might be any other reason to be nice.

We know from the rancor present in the world today that not everyone understands "what goes around comes around". They fail to see that being mean spirited earns them the same in return. They also don't notice the inverse is true – that kindness begets kindness. So, the approach of treating others as you would like to be treated is falling on deaf ears.

However, it goes further. Being kind is not for our convenience. It is a moral obligation. We don't need to argue the case for not stealing or killing and it is not just that if you do it, you will be severely punished. We don't steal or kill because it is morally wrong.

Being kind is a moral obligation. Do what is morally right and be kind to everyone, friend or foe.

The song, "Let there be Peace on Earth" ends with "and let it begin with me."

At a time when there is so much turmoil and unrest, it will take each of us to consider our own individual responsibility to promote peace. Since time immemorial it has always been the "one" that determines our future. While we are a world of innumerable peoples, it is the "one" that makes the difference since these innumerable masses of humanity are collectively made up of "one's".

To change this turmoil and unrest, let there be peace on earth and let it begin with each one of us individually. We can do this.

"Entitlement" is the belief that one is inherently deserving of special treatment or privileges, and it is a notion helping to drive this nation apart.

So where does this notion stem from? The root of entitlement is selfishness, and this selfishness is spread through the media and championed by some people in government. Both the media and government want us to feel entitled because it makes us beholden to them. When they feed these carnal desires, it only makes matters worse.

People don't need the media and government peddling entitlement attitudes – we are pretty good at it ourselves.

With politics, we too often see everything as a one or zero problem. We live in a democracy where the majority decides the outcome, and when we are split on an issue, it becomes the conundrum.

Immigration is one of the most hotly debated topics today. Everyone seems to have an opinion on this topic. Some want to prevent illegal entrance into the country. Others desire no restrictions for entry. And another camp wants to update, modify, and/or correct existing immigration policy.

It is the third one that I want to address. The sticky bit is that there is no consensus on how to best change immigration policy. Most everyone agrees that the policy needs changing but this is where it comes to a grinding halt.

Anytime an issue is not clearly one way or another, the rub begins. Understanding this is crucial to getting along with each other. Remembering we live in a democracy is important. You may not agree with the majority, but you did agree to abiding by the rules of a democratic government.

Don't expect things to go your way if you are not clearly in the majority. You live in one of the best and greatest countries on earth for a reason. Abide and live by the rules and you will be the happier for it.

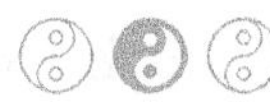

Whether you die rich or poor it makes no difference: you can't take any of your possessions with you.

I read recently a lamentation by Steve Jobs of Apple fame. He wrote it just before he passed away. The crux of his final thoughts were that wealth isn't what makes you happy. Happiness comes from good friends, good health, and good family.

Job's says the best doctors are:

Sunlight, Rest, Exercise, Diet, Self Confidence, Friends

Something to ponder.

Sunday, or the Sabbath, is defined as a day of religious observance where no work is to be performed. While we seem to respect the "no work" aspect of the day, the "religious observance" part has largely fallen into disuse. According to surveys, only around 7% of the U.S. population attends any religious service on the Sabbath, down precipitously from previous generations. Why is this?

I believe that we have become more callused toward religious worship. While over 50% of us say we are religious, we frankly have no desire or need for the formal activity. This seems somewhat of an oxymoron if we say we are religious and yet have no desire to attend services on the Sabbath. How can we truly consider ourselves faithful?

There are significant benefits to us and our families when we do truly and fully observe the Sabbath day. In such rituals, we are reminded and taught about living a good and moral life; to be kind, tolerant, virtuous, forbearing, and honest. Our country can use a huge dose of these teachings today. It would serve us well.

Why are we becoming so polarized on so many issues? I have been giving this some serious thought lately. For most people, their world view comes primarily from the media. Maybe, just maybe the feeling of polarization is being exaggerated by the media to boost ratings.

While there may be some extreme divisions between the hard right and left, I am hoping that the majority of us are not so polarized. This, I hope, is the case or we are in serious trouble as a nation. Are we the silent majority? Maybe we ought not to stay so silent.

There is a saying, "the idle mind is the devil's workshop". When people have nothing to do, they get into trouble; crime increases. When you put in a good day's work, you are more inclined to go home, be with the family and less likely to get into trouble. If we want to improve our society and reduce crime, we need to stop fostering wholesale government assistance and put people to work. In other words, rather than giving them a handout, give them a job.

Giveaways never work -- they breed discontent.

The classic American sense of self-reliance comes to mind when one sees so much of our country living off and dependent on government assistance. For much of our history there were no government handouts. If you didn't work, you didn't fare very well.

We seem to have lost the ability to be self-reliant. It may be that wholesale government assistance reduces the need or desire to be self-reliant. While I was in Singapore several years ago, I was struck with the fact that everyone was working. The city was very clean. I saw no homeless. They found a different way.

It is clear to me why we have so much difficulty achieving compromise in Congress.  It is based in a complete lack of respect for each other. In fact, it is really an utter contempt.

Can there and is there some reasonable middle ground to be had? I say, emphatically, yes! We all can see it, so why can't they? It is my belief that there can be no compromise, no middle ground, as long as there is so much animosity, dislike, and utter contempt for each other.

Come on guys, stop this nonsense. Take a time out and sit down for at least one day and talk nice to each other. Find something good to say about one another. Hold a joint press conference and only say good things and how you can find common ground to build on. You can do this! Give it a try.

Should the U.S. limit legal immigration? Probably not. Should we enforce our current immigration laws? Absolutely!

The "problem" that has resulted in a dire government shutdown has to do with an alleged need for immigration reform. Assuming we already have a good immigration policy, why the need for reforms? Here is some background to help you understand the issue.

1.  For more than 200 years, cheap foreign labor has been brought in, both legally and illegally, to perform menial tasks that domestic labor would not do. We, frankly, have come to expect and depend on this documented and undocumented labor force to perform this work. Old habits are hard to break.

2.  We have been trying for at least 100 years, to protect our borders from illegal immigration. I can remember working on my father's cattle ranch in Southern California, 65 years ago, where we had both documented and undocumented workers on the ranch. The workers would have spotters watching for the Border Patrol and warn the undocumented workers to hide. It was very difficult for the Border Patrol to round up these illegals, but they tried.

3.  For centuries, the U.S. has been a very attractive place to work and with our large and unsecured borders, it is very easy to enter the U.S. illegally. Even though you would think that the aliens should or do know it is illegal to cross the border illegally, the rewards are simply too attractive to ignore. The reward is greater than the risk of getting caught.

Just because so many people break the law, and some don't seem to care doesn't mean we should stop enforcing the law. If we did stop enforcing laws, chaos would ensue. Finding better ways to control illegal immigration is still the answer. Finding ways to provide some form of limited amnesty for qualified illegal immigrants should be considered.

We are a nation governed by laws that are enacted by and for the people. Congress needs to be reminded of this from time to time. It is especially incumbent upon elected officials to abide by our laws since they are the employees of the people that elected them.

Anarchy, on the other hand, is the condition in which a society, group of people, an entity, or an individual rejects the "rule of law". Anarchists only follow laws with which they agree. This is the sad state in which we are headed.

The term "united" means we are unified in our goals and aspirations; hence, the United States. I ask you, are we "united"? Do we have the same aspirations? While we may not all agree on and have the same end goals, we did agree on majority rule and being willing to go along with the majority.

Our articles of incorporation, our Constitution, clearly state that we are to be a country of laws agreed upon by a majority. It is our duty to obey these laws whether or not we personally agree with them so long as these laws do not interfere with rights and freedoms prescribed in our constitution.

To be "law abiding" is to be united.

It is clear to me why we have so much difficulty achieving compromise in Congress.  It is based in a complete lack of respect for each other. In fact, it is really an utter contempt.

How good are you? No, not how capable you are but how good of a person are you? To be a good person is more important. So here is my list of what I believe constitutes a good person. It starts with being:

- Kind
- Caring
- Thoughtful
- Helpful

- Considerate

And continues with:


- Putting others before themselves
- Not using condescending or vulgar language
- Always remaining respectful of others regardless of
  race, religion, gender, political affiliation, or social
  status.

We need more good people in this country. Are you one of
them?

In life, there are two opposing forces: goodness and evil. These
opposing forces are there for a reason. They are a
contradiction for the purpose of helping us understand and
appreciate the differences.

Evil is associated with envying, strife, selfishness, harboring
unkind feelings toward others, animosity, corruptness,
dishonesty, breaking the law, and the list goes on.

Goodness is associated with love, temperance, patients,
honesty, integrity, unwavering respect for others, kindness,
genteelness, and this list goes on.

These two, evil and goodness cannot exist at the same time.
You cannot simultaneously be both good and evil. You can be
good and then be evil, or vice versa. Evil can trump goodness
if allowed to prevail, and goodness can rally to overcome evil.

Being good or evil is a choice we make every hour of every day. We all make mistakes because of our human natures. But we can get back on the goodness train if we work at it consistently, perpetually. Be a goodness advocate and ride this train.

There is good and the bad in almost everything. It is our choice on to which we focus. The news media appears to focus more on the bad in life than the good.

Left unchecked, the media's preference for broadcasting the bad in life can cause us to also lose focus on the good in life, but only if we let it. When this happens, we then become soured, tainted with the belief that life sucks. Is it any wonder then that our children grow up with this attitude? I believe this may be the reason we see a less loving society today.

The question is can this be reversed? The answer is "yes" if each of us decides to end this awful cycle. Let each of us make a resolution to focus more on the "good" this coming year. Please join me and we can reverse this descending spiritual spiral.

# Life

Getting the most out of life is basically two things: serving others and not wasting time.

Being happy when things are not going your way is a true art form. It takes a sincere attitude adjustment that is rare in most people.

So, what is this rare attitude adjustment? Simply put, it is thinking of others before self. It starts with stopping yourself from complaining. Yes, stop yourself from complaining completely.

Complaining is just another nasty habit we acquired when we were just babies/kids. I want what I want when I want it. Some people just love to complain. It is like a drug. It makes them feel good, but other people don't appreciate it. No one likes a complainer.

Stop complaining and make everyone happy, including you.

The best way to learn is to open your ears and shut your mouth.

Some of us get angry and upset when we lose our job. It has been my experience that losing one's job can be a blessing.

Most of us get somewhat complacent in our job. We hate change and thus won't take the time to explore other opportunities to better our future. Getting fired causes us to look elsewhere. It gives us a chance to reflect on what and where we want to go next. Most often this forced change is better than the old job.

Don't fear being fired. It can work out for the best. It did for me.

I can't change your mind, but you can!

If you think success, one of two things will happen. You'll either become successful or just dream about being successful.

Is hope born out of despair?

"Hope" is the desire or expectations for something to happen. Hope deepens when the desire or expectation becomes extremely important to us. Usually, this extreme importance is enhanced when we are in despair or in dire need for something to come to pass. When life is rosy and everything is going our way, we tend to ignore or seem to place less importance on hope.

It seems that "hope" only becomes important when we are in dire straits. This is not only a shame but a tragedy. The feeling

of hope should not just be born out of despair but out of a
desire to improve our future.

If you don't control your emotions, your emotions will control
you.

When hardship and strife dominate our lives, we need to do a
deep dive as to why.

In many cases it may be because we are so preoccupied with
our own dilemma that we can't envision the light at the end of
the tunnel. While it rains challenges on our lives at times,
know this: these things too shall pass. If we focus on the many
good things that are happening to us, it will bring a smile to
our face and help us to endure the storm until the sun once
again appears.

"Put up your dukes," was often said when getting ready to
defend yourself.

We have danger all around us. We need to be ready to defend
ourselves. To defend ourselves doesn't just refer to a threat of
our life, it can mean to avoid insidious threats that can ruin
our lives: such as pornography, bad habits, drugs, and other
similar  threats to our  mental and physical health.

Keep yourself protected against these worldly evils by
"putting up your dukes".

A friend was lamenting that it is hard to be grateful when things don't turn out as expected.

It is difficult to be thankful and happy when important things are not going as we had hoped. While this is perfectly natural to feel less grateful during difficult times, we can improve our attitude by focusing less on the negative outcomes and more on all the things that are going right.

This is counting our blessings not our trials.

Studies show that once a child reaches 15 years, they have extreme difficulty shedding their accent.

I believe this same could apply to character development, in that a person's character is established by their middle teens.

This is why it is so important that children's proper moral compass be set before they become teenagers.

When there is sunshine in your soul, you turn despair into joy.

When our souls are filled with sorrow, let the sunshine in. We will view trials and tribulations differently. Just like when the sun is out and we feel its warmth, sunshine in our soul will bring us the same feeling.

Let the sunshine in and the shadows of darkness will disappear.

Where is your blind spot?

A blind spot is a location in our vision that prevents us from seeing certain things. It can inhibit our ability to recognize important things that should be in our vision. Things like serving those in need. Recognizing a bias that should be corrected. A health issue that should be addressed. A character flaw that needs attention. And this list goes on.

Blind spots that need revealing can slow down our progression if left unattended. Recognizing and resolving blind spots can enrich our lives and increase our joy and happiness.

Let us look back from the future to see what we have become rather than waiting until the future becomes the present.

Our future is determined now by our daily actions and decisions. If we carefully plan and prepare for our future, it will be filled with joy and happiness.

Your future is not long before you. It is in the now that you hold your future. Waste not and you will not regret.

Adversity brings joy, but only when we have overcome the adversity.

Coping and hoping is how we deal with life's challenges.

Coping is the action we take to deal with the challenge while hoping is the way we deal with the stress of the challenge.

Having a positive attitude is the most important aspect of dealing with the vicissitudes of mortality.

Researchers and physicians have found there is a prescription you can fill yourself. This self-administered prescription is simple, and it works.

Spend quality time in nature. Getting outdoors has been found to lower blood pressure, reduce  anxiety and stress which in turn helps you become healthier.

Find time to enjoy nature and be healthier and happier.

As I ponder the travails of mortality, I am reminded of the need to pivot.

Just like in business good companies must learn to pivot. Likewise, as individuals we need to learn the same pivoting skills.

Back in 1994, I lost my vision and became legally blind. This required me to pivot, and pivot I did. I actually became a better person once I pivoted from the dire medical situation that I faced.

We will all have similar types of difficulties in our lives that will require us to do some pivoting. To that I say, learn to pivot or face a difficult future.

"Don't cast your pearls before swine." This saying refers to primarily not wasting your life or your time.

Our life and our time are precious, and we need to treat it that way.

Although we are the same person we were when we were born, we change over time.

Growing up, aging, and experience changes us. Just like ageless music and fine art we can become a classic.

To become a true classic, we need to seek for classic values like honesty, integrity, virtue, kindness, respect for others, productive, helpful, empathic, and loyal.

Seek to be classic with all its virtues and lasting values.

Bad judgment comes from ignorance, good judgment comes from experience.

"Blame" is the result of not accepting responsibility for our actions.

We have the freedom to choose what we do but we do not have the freedom to decide the outcome. There are always consequences for our (in)actions that we cannot escape.

Pleasure or instant gratification is happiness.

But greater happiness comes from delayed gratification; it is longer lasting and is of more value.

We have all heard the saying, "all comes to them that wait". This is "delayed gratification". Wanting or desiring instant gratification can lead to poor decisions and heartbreak. But letting time work its miracle can more often lead to the promise of a delayed gratification that will bring true happiness.

Your past does not necessarily define your future. It may influence your future but that's all.

Your future is primarily defined by your daily actions. If these show promise for change for the better, then your future will reflect this, and the opposite is true if you don't.

Your future is in your hands. You are not a victim of your circumstances. You own your future, not someone else and don't believe otherwise.

If you think you're good, you most likely aren't humble.

If you aren't humble, you most likely aren't teachable.

If you aren't teachable you won't be good.

Our lives are a series of decisions we make every single day.

While there are twists and turns along the way, these daily decisions we make determine who we are and what we will amount to as we proceed down this journey of life. Make no mistake about this, no matter how young or old we are, our daily decisions define us now and into the future.

Choose wisely every single day or you will have serious regrets. We cannot turn back the clock.

Stay optimistic when the clouds of adversity loom the darkest.

First off, if it is under your control – you will fix it given time.

Second, if it is outside your control, there is nothing  to stress over so just let be what will be.

Staying positive will not only help you but will help all those around you. It is a matter of loving and dealing with whatever tragedy and adversity comes your way.

The best day of my life is today! I can't enjoy yesterday or tomorrow so I best make the most out of today.

I was recently asked why there is so much evil and bad in the world. This is a good question and caused me to reflect deeply on this.

Depending on whether you are a fatalist or not I have a different view for you to ponder. Believing we live in a perfect world, in that there must be a perfect balance, there must be, as in Newton's law of physics, for every action or force you have in one direction there needs be an equal and opposite action or force in the opposite direction or there would be no movement or progress. For example, the Corona virus or some other negative force, would wipe us out if we didn't take appropriate action to negate the negative force.

Unfortunately, this balance of nature is distasteful at times. But it is this natural balance that allows us to progress. While I am not praying for more problems and adversity, I do accept this as part of living in this perfect world.

To be creative you must be inspired.

While inspiration often comes at the most unexpected ways and time, to be truly inspired requires regular quiet thinking and pondering. In other words, you must seek inspiration. Only then will you become creative.

The best things in life are not necessarily free. They take dedication and sacrifice.

To get the most out of life is to learn to do the "Tough Things First" everyday (which is the title of my bestselling book). It is all about putting discipline in our lives. To most people, "discipline" is a drudgery that they want to avoid.

This is where dedication and sacrifice come into play. Dedication and sacrifice do not seem appealing or fun, but it is the best way to get the most out of our time here in mortality.

Distress, sorrow, anguish, anxiety are all negative emotions resulting from physical or emotional problems.

These are very personal feelings that are experienced individually. While they can be shared, they can only be experienced personally. Each of us suffers them in different ways.

These negative emotions are usually felt much more deeply than positive emotions and usually last longer. If not controlled, suicide can result.

This is why we try to avoid or suppress them. It is difficult to avoid negative emotions so we will use medication/drugs and distractions to control them. What we want to avoid is using anger and other forms of violence to distract or mitigate negative emotions.

It is our "desire" not our "capacity" that limits us. We also fall short of our capability because of "fear".

Desire and fear become two of our biggest obstacles to success. We view mole hills as mountains. Fear stifles faith in our ability to succeed. We yearn to be successful but lack the confidence to do so.

Take that leap of faith and just go for it.

In life we usually get what we deserve but not necessarily what we want.

If you take control of your life, you'll never be a victim.

As humans, we are either acting or being acted upon. Being acted upon is being a victim.

The world would change your outward behavior by forcing change inward.

To affect your outward behavior, you need to change your inward behavior without being forced to do so. It is this inward change that is longer lasting. Being forced to change is not habit forming and is short lived. Taking this deep dive into our inner self requires serious reflection.

Ask yourself, am I being forced to change? If so, kickback and figure out what needs to change and then fix it.

The choices we make every day determine our happiness or sadness. I have three suggestions that will help you have a more successful and happy life.

1. Take a longer view of your choices: Remember that "what comes around, goes around". It is like comparing instant gratification with delayed gratification. Be patient. Avoid things that only bring you instant gratification.

2. Know your enemies: There is a saying, "keep your friends close and your enemies even closer". Bad choices will come back to bite you.

3. We all make mistakes, but do we all learn from our mistakes? Learning from our mistakes is called "change". Making the same mistake over and over and expecting a different result is insanity. Don't be insane, just change.

"The best is yet to come." We all look forward to a brighter future. This is what gives us hope.

A movie I like is "Back to the Future". It was time travel and going back into the past. With hindsight being 20-20, it suggested the ability to travel back into our past to redo things we didn't like sounds great. But in the movie, it turns out that changing the past affects the future and the outcome would be much different than we really want it to be knowing where we are now.

There are some things that we wish we could change in our past, but we are where we are. "Yesterday is history, tomorrow is a mystery, today is a present, that's why they call it a gift."   Make today the best day and you won't have to retreat back to the past to change it.

Adversity is the engine that drives learning. Without adversity, we lack the motivation to overcome it.

We humans deplore change because it means we have to deal with it. When adversity comes, we are more likely to deal with the changes it brings. Additionally, the one thing we hate more than change is pain. Pain is a major compliment of adversity. This pain that we get through adversity drives us to change.

There is an important saying that goes "no pain no gain". If we feel no pain, then what is the real value of adversity? We need pain to change.

During the mid-1800s there was a mad rush to find gold. People were insanely focused on striking it rich.  Now that those gold-rush days are over, all that's left of that era are abandoned and rundown gold mining towns.

This is an example of how our lives can be when we focus on things that don't have lasting value, such as material possessions. When we turn our focus toward things that never fall out of favor such as serving and helping others, we are truly rich, and our lives become all the more blessed for it.

Do you overcome adversity or does adversity overcome you?

The measure of a person is directly related to how well they deal with adversity. All of us, every single person living on earth has to cope.

How we cope varies.

Do you look at adversity as a hindrance or an opportunity to grow and learn?

During troubled times, where do you turn for peace and where is your solace? Do you lash out and blame others for your troubles and  anxieties? Is this how you get your peace and solace?

If so, you will not get that lasting peace you need and strive for. Being angry and upset will not change most things in life. Real peace and solace only come when you realize that you can't fix everything and instead look on the bright side.

Look for the good things and blessings you already enjoy. Be happy and peace will be in your life through thick and thin.

When things don't happen in the way and time you want them to, just chock it up to being like everyone else. That is just life.

We human beings are not just "being" but "becoming".

Our lives are not static but dynamic. We are either progressing or retrogressing. With all our daily doings, we need to focus on how these doings are benefiting what we are becoming.

It is what we are becoming that will determine our degree of success in life. To engage in life's true meaning of becoming a successful human being, focus on what it takes and that is looking outward, not inward.

Life is to be enjoyed, not wasted.

Are you happy? Do you feel fulfilled whether you are having a "good" day or "bad"?

It is not hard to enjoy good days. It is those bad days that we find more challenging. That being said, bad days are almost as frequent as good days and thus wanting to be happy everyday will necessitate us having the proper perspective regarding bad days.

It is that virtual making "lemonade out of lemons" – finding the silver lining in every storm that besets us. Being an optimist in every bad day.

I am reminded about the story of the parents that filled their young son's room with horse manure for Christmas in an effort to tone down his optimism. The parents were awakened Christmas morning with loud and boisterous noises coming from their son's room. Upon opening the door to their son's room, they were astonished with all the horse manure flying around.

The parents then shouted, "hey son, what's going on in here"? The little boy's head then popped up out of the manure and gleefully exclaimed, "with all this horse manure in here there has to be a pony in here somewhere".

If we will look for the positives when there is so much negative, we too can find those "silver linings amidst those stormy clouds of despair". It is our choice to be happy no matter what challenges of "bad" days we face.

The 2020/21 pandemic drove us all nuts. There were a lot of unknowns and concerns.

Just look at it this way. You should only worry about the things you can change and have the ability to do so. Other than that, wringing your hands and getting upset won't change a darn thing.

Keep this whole mess in perspective. You are not alone, and things will get better very soon.

What will your obituary say?

An obituary is a summary of your life when you pass away. It will list all of your achievements and accomplishments. It will be your legacy. Hopefully, your obituary will sum up a very successful life.

You should be thinking about it now before it is too late.

In the children's book, "Alice's Adventures in Wonderland" there is an exchange between Alice and the Cheshire cat that I really enjoy.

Alice comes to a fork in the road and asks the cat, "which road should I take?" The cat then says, "that depends on where you want to go." Alice then says, "I don't know." The cat then retorts, "well then, it doesn't much matter which road you take."

We all face "forks in the road" as we venture through life. These "forks in the road" come as challenges or decisions we face every day. Knowing where you are heading or the direction you want to take will make the choice of which "fork" to take all that much easier.

Unfortunately, we are often confused or lackadaisical about where we are headed or want to go. We figure that all roads lead to somewhere and if we travel long enough, we will see where it ends up. While this may appear adventurous it can be very treacherous if the destination isn't really where we want to be.

If you want to get the most out of life, take control and know the path that will get you there the fastest and safest.

Are things really changing at a faster pace than ever before?

Having lived over 3/4 of a century, I have doubts. I believe the issue has more to do with us humans resisting change. While we love progress and an improved standard of living, we want to see all of this without having to deal with the change. I call this the Rip van Winkle phenomena. In this 1816 story, Rip van Winkle wanders into the mountains with his trusty dog to escape his wife. He finally returns to civilization some 100 years later and is surprised at how much things have changed since he left.

Are we like Rip van Winkle, where we want change but don't want deal with it? Life would get pretty boring without change. I have a sister who hates change so much she refuses to use many of our modern conveniences such as cell phones and computers.

Some of us love the technological improvements and have no issue with change while others don't. For as long as we live here in mortality, change will be ever with us.

Learn to accept and enjoy change and you will be the happier for it.

Does tragedy work for our good?

Some say that nothing good comes from tragedy. The tragedy erupting from the current pandemic is an example of how tragedy can work for our good. We will learn to keep ourselves healthier, learn how to work in a virtual environment, develop closer family ties, serve one another better, develop better therapeutics, and so much more.

Rather than only look at tragedy as a hopeless peril, let's look tragedies as a necessary element to help us improve.

Self-reliance should be the goal and objective of all of us. This means to have the following:

1.  A viable source of providing the needs of ourselves and family.
2.  A sufficient savings to sustain us through difficult times.
3.  Sufficient food storage to sustain us during a crisis.
4.  A regular exercise routine.
5.  Eat regular and nourishing meals.
6.  A good night's rest, usually 8 hours per night.
7.  Self-improvement like a good education.

Live happy and be happy by being self-reliant.

When we worry about things we can't change, we change our outlook of the future. We become more pessimistic and less optimistic.

To get more enjoyment out of life we need to change our view of the future. This means we have to stop worrying about things we can do nothing about.

When things currently look bad it only means that the future looks bright. This is because things don't stay bad forever.

Sometimes the worst fights are the ones we have with ourselves. It can get downright ugly. It can be highly emotional.

Just like we can be our own worst enemy, we can also be our worst critic.

My advice is not to get too down on yourself. This can be devastating if we don't control it. It is okay to review and critique dumb decisions but not to dwell on them. This is just being honest with ourselves to insure we don't repeat the mistake.

When we drink from the bitter cup of adversity, we are prone to be angry and say, "why me, why do I deserve this?"

Adversity and challenges are going to be a regular occurrence in our lives. They are there because it is what happens in mortality.

Adversity has an important purpose: it helps us grow. Like fertilizer that helps our gardens grow, these challenges are fertilizer in our life.

If we can learn to accept these life challenges as the best way to help us grow and improve, it will go a long way to help us deal with these difficult circumstances.

It is by and through pure and simple things that bring us the most joy in life. Don't complicate your life. Be satisfied and enjoy what you have: family and friends.

The story of "Little Orphan Annie" deals with the struggles of children in an orphanage. The children were losing hope for any improvement in their dire situation. Dressed in rags with little food to nourish their impoverished bodies, they felt helpless and alone.

Annie spent her time trying to bolster the spirits of the children. She offered them hope by encouraging them "tomorrow, tomorrow, there is always tomorrow".

When the shadows of darkness envelope around us and we feel the gloom of despair, know this, there is always tomorrow and tomorrow will come.

During my tenure as CEO of Micrel, we went through eight significant downturns in the 37 years I ran the company. After each downturn, we emerged even stronger and healthier. "That which does not kill you makes you stronger." It is like when we break a bone, it mends even stronger.

Having hope is the Achilles' heel to disasters. Just hope for a brighter tomorrow and you will emerge all the better.

The highs and lows of life is what makes mortality interesting.

Without these differences, we could not enjoy the sweetness that comes along when things are going well. While none of us appreciate the times when things are not going well, we tend to learn more from those experiences that try our patience.

So why do we stew and fret over things outside our purview and control?

I think it is exactly because it is outside our purview and control that we fret and stew. This is the boogeyman syndrome. We are worried that things we can't see or control that worry  us. It is those things that go bump in the night that gets our adrenaline up. It is the fear of the unknown.

Instead of hoping for the best and planning for the worst, we don't hope at all for fear of being disappointed. We focus so much on expecting, not planning for the worst, that we lose all hope.

Let us get back to hoping for the best and plan/being prepared for the worst. In so doing you have all your bases covered and you will live a happier and more productive life.

What do you have that no one else has? Your free agency. It is this agency that determines who and what you are.

So, make the best of this treasure and only make the best decisions and you will be the happier for it. Think carefully before you act and save yourself a lot of regrets.

The ups and downs of mortality is just a fact of life.

Even though we know this, we still get bent out of shape when things don't go like we want. Since it seems that half the time things are not going as well as we would like, we are in a bad mood half the time.

We would all like to be in a better mood more often, so my suggestion is we learn to accept and appreciate life even when things aren't going well. We need to say to ourselves more often, "well that's just life". Just let it go and move on.

Just come what may and be happy.

What is your claim to fame?

We all have a purpose here in mortality. To get the most out of our life we need to discover our special purpose.

To help you figure out your special calling, ask a good friend or family member what they think you are good at. Once you have it clearly in mind, build upon this talent.

"Life can be like fighting an uphill battle" or "It seems like you can't win for losing".

Both are a defeatist view of life. When you get to feeling like this, you need to step back, take a deep breath and count your blessings.

You really do have blessings. You are just being caught up in a bunch of problems that seem to overwhelm you at the moment. When you honestly reflect on how really blessed you are, the problems of the moment will tend to disappear.

Some say that life is no bowl of cherries. But it can be just as sweet and delicious if we have the right outlook on life. It is all a matter of "your" perspective.

Adversity is like drinking nasty tasting medicine, it's hard to swallow but can be good for you.

Prayer is music for the soul. It calms the troubled heart. It lifts our spirits. When we pray, we are not alone. It comforts us and gives us solace.

In times of tribulation, pouring out our hearts can help us deal with almost any difficulty. Pray often and you will be at peace.

"Making hay while the sun shines" means the hay you harvest will not be moldy when it is baled.

There is the right time for everything. If it isn't the right time, things can turn out very ugly.

We have passions. But is that "passion" getting us to where we need to go?

A passion is a powerful driving force that needs to be properly directed. Misdirected passions are often futile or even dangerous.

Examine your passion. Make sure it is a good one that will not only elevate you but those around you.

Rolling with the punches is a boxing term. If a boxer sees an unavoidable blow coming to their head, instead of resisting, they let their head "roll" and thus absorb less of a shock.

In life this means to not let bad things take us down. Rolling with life's punches requires that we understand the problems facing us and recognize that we cannot always control the outcome.

Roll with life's punches and "these things too shall pass".

If the sun doesn't shine in your life, don't blame the weather. It is your attitude that determines the amount of sunshine you feel.

Is any New Year going to be a good year? This all depends on your point of view.

If you are hoping this year is going to be better than the last, then you will be looking for the positives and just the opposite if you are not hopeful. This is where our attitude plays a part in how we view the outcome of certain events. We all see things in accordance with our viewpoint. Whether we are hopeful or not will not change the course of the events.

This reminds me of when my wife isn't happy with the way certain people are driving and expresses her frustration out loud in the car. This is when I will reply, "I am sure they heard you".

You can be happy or unhappy with the way certain events play out but that won't change the outcome. My suggestion is not to let events you can't control determine your attitude. As in the song, "Que sera, sera", whatever will be will be. Like the water off a duck's back, don't let it get under your skin and you will be the happier for it.

In an instant our lives can change and tragically so.

Bad things do happen to good people. A friend and his wife were involved in an accident last night and the wife was killed.

We never know what is just around the corner for us. We need to be grateful for the moments when things appear to be going well.

To make lemonade out of lemons is a real challenge at times. None of us like to be inconvenienced or disappointed. It's difficult to smile in the face of adversity.

To deal with these challenges, we can only grin and bear it.

Do you have perspicacity? If you do, then you have a very keen and honed vision. You have great insight. You are perceptive with understanding of how certain things work.

Perspicacity can only come through good wisdom and judgement. It is an attribute that should be keenly sought after.

When we think things can't get any worse, they usually do.

In life we never hit bottom when we think we do. The reason for this is that the bottom is in the future and since we can't predict the future, we speculate that things can't get worse.

Rather than wringing our hands worrying about the situation we are in, buck up and deal with it. Make lemonade out of those lemons. There is always a silver lining in any difficulty or challenge we face.

So rather than stew about it, go find that silver lining. It is there just waiting for you to tap into it.

There is a pot of gold at the end of every rainbow in life. It all has to do with our attitude.

It is our hope that determines our attitude. The greater our hope the better chance we have of finding that pot of gold (happiness) in life. It is amazing how our attitude influences our view of life.

The happier and more optimistic we are, the bigger is that pot of gold at the end of the rainbow (our life).

When you have any hatred or animosity toward anyone, you will become less and less effective as a person.

These negative emotions wear you down and prevent you from accomplishing much at all.

"Today while the sun shines, work with a will, today while the sun shines, your duty fulfill".

This line comes from a song that I sing which speaks to the need of "making hay while the sun shines".

Get the most out of your day while you have the health and the energy to do it.

A line from Shakespeare's Macbeth reads, "This life ... is but a walking shadow; a poor player, that struts and frets his hour upon the stage, and then is heard no more."

Life can seem hopeless  and shallow if viewed this way. We all come into mortality knowing there is a finite beginning and end.

This is all the more reason to make the best of it regardless of how long or short your life may be. Don't let the memory of your life be lost. You can linger on long  after you have passed if you make a difference for the better while living.

Envy is morphing into "malignant envy".

Coveting things is an age old negative human characteristic. It is the desire to have something that others have. Envying has always been a serious disease, but it seems to be developing new strains.

If envy becomes malignant, just like cancer, it can consume an entire being. They become so absorbed by the disease that they become irrational and will do anything, illegal or not, to get what they want.

To avoid this disease, you will need to never let envy take root to begin with. Be satisfied with what you have and applaud others if they have something you don't.

I have been reminded how readily our problem past can come back to haunt us. Our past is never really forgotten. This brings up a good point. There is a saying that goes, "forgive and forget". While it is encumbered upon all of us to forgive others their trespasses, it is better to seek forgiveness quickly so our past will not come back to haunt us later on in life.

We cannot hide our past, even though many of us try. Hiding anything is never good. The best way to get rid of your past is to handle it in the present.

"Faith" promotes "learning".

We do not  possess all knowledge. Hence, faith becomes the vehicle to help us learn. Skepticism, which is the opposing factor in having faith and will restrict our learning.

I am not proposing we should have "blind" faith but rather "educated" faith. This educated faith is to have hope in things we wish for but not having conclusive evidence of its validity. In this manner, our learning will be enhanced because we will not waste time questioning everything.

Go forward in faith and your learning will increase.

We live in a dynamic world. If we are not progressing, we are retrogressing.

If we choose to progress, we need to focus daily on doing better. Progression is a step-by-step  daily effort. This involves not wasting so much time on trivial pursuits. We all know what time wasters are, so spend little or no time doing these activities no matter how appealing they may be.

Your choice, progress or retrogress. Time stops for no man or woman.

Work quietly and systematically toward those things that will lead and guide you in the pursuit of happiness.

If you get mad or upset remember that it was your decision.

The tongue is a small organ that can cause a lot of damage. Keep that small organ under control and you will have less damage to deal with.

Life holds many uncertainties of mortality.

Because of this, life can be trying at times. The optimist takes these ups and downs in stride. The pessimist, on the other hand, looks for the next downturn rather than enjoying the upturn while they have it.

Optimism is the only way to enjoy life.

Want to lower your blood pressure? Try lowering your voice and think more positively about life.

Are we just too preoccupied to smell the roses?

In a recent study, a world-famous violinist, dressed in casual clothes, was positioned at a busy subway station in New York City. He was playing some very difficult music on a Stradivarius violin, worth millions of dollars, and only seven people out of 1100 even noticed him.

This may explain why we have become so callous. Life is more than getting what we want when we want it. You can't fully appreciate the beauty of this world unless you take time to smell the roses.

The cost of a college education is skyrocketing beyond what many people can afford. Taking on massive student debt may not be the best answer.

The purpose of a college education is to improve one's chances of greater income over their life. Not factoring in the repayment of student loans is a mistake, but especially so if the enhancement to your income does not cover this added monthly repayment expense.

Given the time spent obtaining a college degree, compounded by when the debt incurred is greater than the return, serious consideration should be given to other means such as trade schools or extension classes.

If you do go to college, make sure the degree you seek provides the best chances for continuous and profitable work. In today's and tomorrow's workplace, the best opportunities are in manufacturing, financial, health care, and IT.

Changing jobs can be both a benefit and a hindrance. If you're considering changing employers, consider the following:

1) Don't be a chain-job-changer. Changing jobs every couple of years is viewed negatively.

2) Don't make a move unless the total compensation is at least 20% more than you are currently making.

"Better the devil you know than the devil you don't know".

What is "truth"? Is truth only true if we agree with it?

Unfortunately, this appears more and more to be the case. Truth no longer has to be fact based. In the past to search for truth, we would do exhaustive research in the library going through numerous sources that have gone through rigorous fact checking. Whereas today we rely on internet searches which may or may not have gone through rigorous fact checking.

Searching for the "truth" in today's internet environment will require careful exploring of the subject so not to get mislead. A careful understanding of the reliability of the source being used is crucial. Just because the source agrees with your perspective doesn't mean you have the "truth".

There is an old saying, "don't confuse me with the facts because my mind is made up already". This, unfortunately, seems to be too often how we come to our "truth". Don't be fooled by your view of the truth if your mind has already decided what the truth is. To avoid this, ask yourself, am I truly, truly open to the truth no matter where it leads me?

In the center of an airplane control panel there is an instrument called the attitude indicator.

The proper attitude when for an airplane is the indicator show blue is up and the brown is down (sky and earth) . In life it is the same. You always want to have the right attitude, or you just might crash.

Just like in flying, our attitude makes all the difference in getting us safely where we are going. Be safe by having the right attitude.

They say that repeating the same mistake and expecting a different result is insanity. So then, why do we keep making the same mistake over and over if we are not insane?

I don't think we expect a different result. I just think we are being stupid. Being stupid is making the same mistake and knowing what will result. Your choice. Stop making the same mistake or look stupid.

Recently a 200-year-old Oak tree came crashing down in our yard. This once gigantic and magnificent tree provided beauty and shade. We loved that tree. Alas but now, it is a huge mess for us to cleanup. What took hundreds of years to grow will be no more in just a matter of days.

This incident reminds me of our lives. What can take years to develop can be in shambles in a matter of days. Don't leave a mess for others to cleanup.

When I was flying after the holidays, I saw the beauty of snowcapped mountains below. Everything was peaceful, quiet.

I wonder why we can't have that same peace that I experience at 40,000 feet when on the ground.

When we are above the fray everything is grandeur and peaceful. Being above the fray is where we all need to be if we were to have peace of mind.

When you get angry or frustrated, are you developing or feeding a bad habit at the same time?

The answer is, yes. While anger and frustration are developed at a very young age, it need not carry into adulthood. Combating these urges is like avoiding the reaction of saying "ouch" when we get hurt.

Maybe we can't totally eliminate being angry or frustrated, but we can strive to minimize feeding this ugly habit. Here's how to begin.

1. Focus on the good in life.
2. Be grateful more than hateful.
3. Speak kindly to and of others.
4. And count to 10 before lashing out.

Life will go on with or without you. However, if you make the most of your life you will be missed.

The two most important things you should do every day is do the Tough Things First and second, tell your family and friends how much you love and appreciate them.

What you take for granted, other people are praying diligently for. Be grateful for all you have and never take anything for granted. You never know when you may be the one praying.

Start today with a smile and your day will be worthwhile.

You never know how good you have it until you don't have it! This is the sad state of any of us who have lost something of value or precious.

I have a friend who was recently in a serious bicycle accident and became a quadriplegic. It happened in an instant. Moments before he was a vibrant and accomplished executive and bicyclist and very independent. Seconds later he became crippled and very dependent on others.

Take nothing precious for granted. Be always grateful. If you do lose something of value, continue to be grateful for what you still have and move on.

The two most important things that will help us deal with tragic circumstances are patience and time. Patience because it helps us to stay optimistic and time because it heals all wounds.

Gamblers are not investors. To gamble is to take a chance on a random event. Don't gamble on your future. Have a strategy that eliminates or at least reduces the chance for failure.

Life is like a mirror. It reflects everything it sees. What is your mirror reflecting? Are you happy with your reflection? If not, change.

It is an interesting human characteristic that good habits are hard to start but bad habits are super easy to implement. By the same token, good habits are very easy to stop but bad habits are difficult to terminate.

Ergo, work diligently to develop good habits and work even harder to rid yourself of the bad habits.

"Cutting off one's nose to spite their face" is just plain stupid. Yet, people do it because of pride and anger. In the end, all they do is hurt themselves.

Humility and wisdom help to keep us from doing dumb things. Avoid stupidity. Be smart and think things through well before allowing pride or anger to make decisions for you.

"A word to the wise is sufficient."

This saying makes the point that wise people need not be told something more than once. They get the message and don't need to have a picture painted for them.

Wise people are good listeners. They also listen to and learn from their mistakes, and thus don't repeat them.

You can get all the answers you want, and thus be knowledgeable. But are you wise?

Wisdom is defined as the proper application of knowledge. Wisdom is
worth more than knowledge, and thus should be more sought after.
Gaining knowledge is wonderful but without the wise use of it, knowledge becomes worthless.

Interestingly, when you seek wisdom, more knowledge will follow.

"Busy" and "productive" are not synonyms … or are they? "Busy as a bee" means you are being productive. However, being preoccupied with "busy work" is not.

There is a saying, "If you want to get something done, give it to a "busy" person." People who have a lot on their plate tend to be well organized. The two go hand in hand.

Bottomline is if you find a person who is very productive, they will also be very busy.

You can't win them all, but you can always keep trying. This should be the motto for all successful people.

Let's take a closer look at the meaning of "winning". Winning is when a desirable outcome occurred. Sometimes outcomes are not what you expected, but the end result was better. This is still a win, the making of lemonade out of lemons.

Making the best of a bad situation is a sign of a truly successful person. They are always looking at the bright side of every situation no matter how dire it may be. If you can do this, life will be so much happier and productive.

Petty frustration is a bad habit stemming from selfishness.

To overcome this problem, you need a complete change of heart. Instead of looking at what is going wrong, look at only those things that are going right.

In other words, count your blessings not your petty frustrating issues.

"Oh shoot, I forgot." In our hectic world, we often forget. We just have too many distractions. Even with all of our smart devices, we can forget important things.

My way around this artifact of human shortcoming is to sit down first thing every morning and list all the tasks that need to get done that day. Then I tackle the most difficult tasks first and get them out of the way. I also compare my list with my calendar just to make sure I haven't left out something. I will frequently consult with my wife to see if there is something I may have overlooked.

Get in the habit of double checking your "to do list" and you will find there are very few things you forgot.

The best financial advice is "waste not, want not". The primary reason people get into financial difficulties is because they are not prudent in the way they manage their financial resources: waste being the biggest culprit.

Learning to live within your means takes a lot of discipline. Ask yourself, "do I really need this?" Too often our wants exceed our needs, and we end up underwater financially. It is wasteful when we want something we really don't need. Manage your financial resources well and you will be the happier for it.

The "power of discernment" is a very special skill. It is the ability to understand what to do and say that can keep you out of trouble.

It is that "still small voice" sometimes referred to as one's conscience. It is always there but people don't always listen and heed it. Why do we too often ignore this inner voice?

Because pride gets in the way. We just want what we want, when we want it, even if it will ultimately come back and bite us. So, if you want to avoid being bitten, listen to that "still small voice" we all have within us.

Everyone has a "sweet spot", an area where they perform at optimum level.

Identifying and fine-tuning your sweet spot is what's important. You find and refine that by determining what brings you the greatest joy and satisfaction.

Once you have settled on that thing (or things) that compose your sweet spot(s), nurture it like you would any other precious possession. Perfecting what brings you joy adds contentment to your life.

When is a mistake bad? When it is not corrected.

We all make mistakes, and this is natural, and hopefully we learn through making our mistakes. This is how we progress.

I am not referring to evil or bad decisions. Those kinds of mistakes can be avoided if we make righteous choices. The kinds of mistakes I am referring to are those that happen while learning.  It is hard to avoid making mistakes during any learning process. Liken it to the "bum notes" we make while learning to play a musical instrument.

Don't be afraid of making "learning" mistakes but avoid making bad choices. While this latter group can often be corrected, they none-the-less cause much heartache and pain. Mistakes through learning, yes. Mistakes through sinning, no.

Having nothing productive to do is a terrible waste. Yet we spend countless hours glued to our smart devices. It is estimated that we spend an average of 8 hours per day on our smart phones.

While these devices can be very helpful, they can, at the same time, kill our productivity if we don't use them wisely. Be smart, don't let your smart devices ruin your productivity.

Courage is not being fearless. Courage is pushing through your fears.

Heroes are not born courageous. They have learned to stare difficult challenges in the face, grit their teeth and carry on.

Be a hero! Don't let adversity defeat you.

Overcoming improper thoughts is one of the most difficult battles we all face. Since thought precedes the action, if we can control our thoughts, our actions will turn out a whole lot better.

So how can we control our thoughts? Here are some suggestions.

1) Think of the consequences.

2) Change the topic in your mind; don't dwell on the improper thoughts.
3) Sing a favorite religious song in your mind.
4) Don't watch or listen to subjects that put the improper thoughts in your mind.

Since "wrong" thoughts can ruin your life, control your thoughts before you act upon them.

I have good news, and I have bad news. Which do you want to hear first?"

I always want to hear the good news first. Usually, the good news takes away the sting of the bad.

Nothing in life worth having is free, and in life, there is always good news and bad news. There is always a price to pay for the good things in life. Consequences whether from good actions/news or bad are part of life.

A church song that I like says "Do what is right let the consequence follow, battle for freedom in spirit and might." If you do what is right, everything works out for the good even if there is some bad that comes with it. Don't ever be afraid of doing what's right.

"Some people never learn." We say this when someone continues to make the same mistake over and over. One goal of life is to learn from our mistakes and not repeat them.

Why do some people never learn? They apparently believe that lightning won't strike twice in the same spot, that somehow their prior mistakes won't happen again. But ask any radio tower or a launch pad at Kennedy Space Center. They know that lightning hits the same spot, over and over again.

Repeating the same decision-making process and expecting a different outcome is as suicidal as standing atop a launch pad during a Florida thunderstorm.

Learn from your mistakes. Repeating them invites disaster.

There is no amount of "success" that can compensate for failure in the home.

In today's society, success in business and professional endeavors have resulted in the disintegration of the family. This came from applying too much importance on things outside the home.

If our society is to flourish, a refocused effort on family and home must take precedence. By promoting family, you help ensure the future success of our society.

"I can't win for losing," is an old saying for having too many losing streaks. It seems the losses are greater than the wins.

In truth, this may not be the case. It is just that the losses are more painful and thus we just think we are losing more than we are winning. Statistics show that, on average, our decisions, and thus our win/losses are no better than 50%. Most of our daily choices could be made with a coin toss.

A loss can be turned into a win if you learn something from the loss. What makes us a habitual loser is not learning from our mistakes and repeating them. Those who repeat the past fail in the future.

Be a winner. Learn from your mistakes and never repeat them.

"Intentional misunderstandings" occur when you try not to understand what someone is saying. This is an all-too-common problem, especially between individuals who dislike each other. Just know this: if you are delivering a message, those that do not like you are going to twist anything you say.

It is extremely important that you know and understand your audience if you want your message to be properly interpreted. So how do you deliver a message that your enemies can't misinterpret?

- Avoid controversial subjects or words.

- If you must address a controversial subject or words, make sure you use appropriate examples to illustrate your point. Paint the proper picture.

- Don't come across angry or upset even if you are.

- Tone done the rhetoric or diatribe. Going on and on comes across as argumentative.

- Appear to be "taking the high road". Don't use condemning rhetoric.

- Use a calm voice. Loud voices come across as angry or upset.

- Avoid using flowery or complicated words. These make you appear arrogant.

- Never ever use foul language to make your point. This again will make you appear classless and upset.

Bottomline, a good speaker or communicator is respected, and people are more likely to heed the message.

During the Christmas season I love to listen to music. One song in particular comes to mind.

It is from the Sound of Music, "A Few of My Favorite Things". The part that hits me the most is, "when the dog bites, and the bee stings, and I am feeling sad, I simply remember a few of my favorite things and then I don't feel so bad."

Especially  this Christmas when things seem so bad, I need to focus and remember the many blessings I have had over the years. Focusing on the blessings and other wonderful things that have elevated my life helps me endure the things that are not so pleasant.

So, "when the dog bites and the bee stings, and you are feeling sad, just simple remember a few of your favorite things and then you won't feel so bad".

Compass, *n.*, a device used to guide us and keep us from getting lost.

If the compass is faulty, it will not keep us on the correct path. Some compasses use magnetic north as a standard and never need calibrating. Electronic compasses, such as found on your cell phone, must be calibrated and recalibrated regularly against the standard of true north.

Like these physical devices, we each have an internal compass that guides us through life. It is often referred to as a "moral" compass. The morals that guide us will, in large part, determine where and how we end up in life.

If our internal compass is based on never changing standards, like the magnetic compass, we will unlikely go down the wrong path. On the other hand, if our internal compass is based on ever changing morals, or morals based on our interpretation of morality, we will be like the electronic compass, forever in need of recalibration against the everchanging standards and norms.

We have a choice, to be led by a consistent moral compass or one that changes constantly based on human interpretation what is socially in vogue.

I choose to be led by a never changing moral compass and not one based on the fickle and fragile whims of morality as interpreted by humans.

A wonderful day need not be a day without challenges. A wonderful day can be dealing with those challenges with a smile.

When you feel you want more, odds are you probably have enough. This happens when you are focusing on getting more rather than being satisfied with what you already have.

"Fight or flight" is an instinctive animal behavior. But can this be true for us humans?

Yes. Here's why. When confronted by an adversary with whom we are not afraid, we will "fight", be it arguing or attacking. If on the other hand, we are confronted with an adversary with whom we are intimidated or afraid, we will flee.

This is natural. But are we to act like animals? I don't think so. Unlike animals, we can reason. We consider our options and then take appropriate action. "Appropriate" is the key word here. "Appropriate" means suitable or proper in the circumstance.

Far too often we don't take "appropriate" action. We let the pendulum swing from one extreme to the other. We too often "shoot first and ask questions later." We then are like animals. We react rather than act. We don't take the time to consider the most "appropriate" response. We just let it "fly" and this is when we get into trouble.

We need to learn to control our reaction to the circumstances we face. Stay in control and you will always take the "appropriate" action.

There is a popular song that I like called "Que sera, sera", which means "whatever will be, will be". In the song there are the words "the future is not ours to see, que sera, sera, whatever will be, will be".

While we cannot predict the future, we can influence it by our actions and decisions. I am a strong advocate that we control more of our future then most may believe.

So, if the song is right and "the future is not ours to see", how is it possible to guide our future? We, to a large degree, control our health, our educational endeavor, our profession, our spouse, where we live, our friends, and our lifestyle.

All of these choices determine your future. Make no mistake about it, you do control much of your destiny. Deal with it wisely and you will be the happier for it.

Anger is a burden. It kills our passion to love and respect others.

Anger has no purpose but to remind us of our selfish nature. Overcoming this takes a great deal of self-control.

My mother used to say, "bite your tongue" when I would get angry or upset. Until I could get control of my emotions, I had a very sore tongue.

Fight your urge to be angry and save your tongue.

"Grin and bear it" my mother used to say when I got weighed down with a particulate problem.

So why "grin" when life seems dark and dreary? Try "grinning" sometime when things seem to be falling apart. You will immediately notice how it will pick up your spirits and help you move forward dealing with your dilemma.

"It is what it is" and no matter how much we don't like it, we have to deal with it.

This is the way it is for most everything distasteful and problematic in life. That is why I have emphasized learning to love the things you hate.

Doing the Tough Things First puts in place a disciplined approach to living our lives. It helps us deal with adversity and dealing with adversity is what life is all about.

ANYTHING HELPS

# Humanity

To "prevail" is to be superior or having a greater importance. At this crucial time of our lives, we need to let love and unity prevail.

Kindness is one of our greatness human attributes.

Kindness is giving service without expecting something in return. Kindness is thinking good thoughts when you are being verbally attacked. Kindness is being respectful of others. Kindness is never using vulgar or condescending language. Kindness is always being honest and truthful. Kindness is loving those who despitefully use you.

Kindness is the true essence of greatness.

Are you "mean" or "well-meaning"?

This is a choice we make every day of our lives. Whether we are driving and are concerned with the behavior of other drivers, interacting with others in a store or sports event, our children and spouses, our neighbors, people at work, or our government we need to access our behavior: are we "mean" or "well-meaning".

Help build a better world. Be always "well-meaning".

Overcoming depression during this holiday season is so important.

The holiday season is supposed to be joyous and festive, but it can also be stressful … especially this year.

If you are one those who is stressed this year, find ways to focus on the happy things, the good memories. Reach out to those less fortunate and undergoing more challenges. Getting outside yourself to lift others will help you appreciate what you have.

Years ago, when my daughter was a young teenager, our family went to a homeless shelter to share some gifts with those in the shelter. A girl, at the shelter, about the same age as my daughter, asked my daughter if her family was rich. My daughter was taken back by the question and only said, "no, we are not rich". The young homeless girl then asked my daughter if she had a home. My daughter responded, "yes". Then the homeless girl said, " if you have a home, then you are rich".

This was a very teaching moment for our family. Rather than focus on our own problems and challenges, focus instead on our blessings and turn our stress into being grateful. Happy holidays will follow.

We all need something that acts as our guiding light: a beacon that lights our way.

Finding that beacon of light can be a source of inspiration as we move forward to improve our lives. Make sure that source of inspiration is filled with truth, not just the appearance of truth.

Truth can be found when it feels "right" down deep in our heart, the very bowels of our soul. When truth prevails, you will find that guiding light to enhance your existence and strengthen your progress.

It is our "pride" that separates us from others. "Pride" is an inward focusing attribute that shuts us out from seeing the value in others.

If you shun the need to puff yourself up, you will find yourself drawing closer to others and feeling their love and value.

Where there is love, there is peace. Love and hate cannot coexist. You will have either one or the other.

Hate should have no place in our life. Selfishness is the author of hatred. When we put ourselves first, we are more likely to be selfish and thus not a loving person. We need less selfishness and more caring for the welfare of others.

Help build peace in the world by putting others first.

Hope is the North Star that guides us through life.

Without hope we have no direction. Life needs to be filled with hope. It gives us purpose and direction. We rely on hope to move us with compassion.

Hope fills our life with joy and meaning. It is the lifeblood of our existence.

These days, politics, sports, and business is not just about promoting how good we are but more to do with tearing down the competition. It seems that we like to see people lose more than win. When we watch a car race, we don't just like to root for a winner. We prefer to see the crashes.

Some of the most successful video games are extremely violent. What is this about wanting to see people lose or get hurt? This is in effect, promoting violence. Can we ever turn away from this human propensity for violence? We can but only if stop promoting it.

Just like with any other addiction, we must completely stop wanting and desiring it. We must shun it at all cost. Help stop violence by completely turning away from it.

"Blessed are the peacemakers."

What we need now are more peacemakers, more blessed people.

Rise and shout and remove all fears of doubt. This musing says it all. To live a successful life there are two things to ponder. To have a happy and successful life you must have a good sense of humor and a loving attitude of forgiveness. These two attributes are crucial in dealing with life's challenges and travails.

A good sense of humor will let you smile and be of good cheer no matter how difficult life's challenges may be. You will say, no matter how difficult the obstacles are, "bring it on, I am ready".

Loving  forgiveness will keep you from having a rotten attitude. You will be happy and satisfied because you hold no grudges. You will not have a victim mentality. Forgiveness is the fruit of joy and happiness.

Live longer by having a good sense of humor and a loving attitude of forgiveness. The world needs more of this. Won't you help?

If you think you are great, you are not humble and are looking inward. Greatness is outward facing.

Greatness is not your wealth, prestige, notoriety, or position. Greatness is how others perceive you. It is your kindness, generosity, forgiving nature, tolerance, forbearance, and service to others that makes you great.

Be a "great" person and enhance your existence.

Did you do any good today? Did you cheer up the sad, made someone feel glad? If not, you have failed "in deed".

If our hearts are knit with righteous, unity, and charity we will not harbor any unkind feelings toward anyone regardless of their race, religion, or social status.

On the other hand, if our hearts are knit with hatred, envy, selfishness, judging, and condemning, we cannot have empathy, understanding, and unity for mankind.

We have a choice. Hopefully, you will choose righteousness, unity and charity, and shun hatred, envy, selfishness, judging, and condemning others.

"Tweets" are what songbirds sing and they are usually melodic and sweet.

To "squawk" is to make a sound that is harsh and loud, like a crow and crows are annoying.

It seems to me that when we "tweet" something through social media, it sounds more like a squawk. We need to squawk less and tweet more.

To focus on money and wealth will distract you from more important things of life: friends, family, and serving others.

Having a "good" life is what we all strive for but having a good life doesn't mean there will not be challenges along the way. It just means that being a good person is what we should strive to be.

This is really having a "good" life.

Some of us can feel alone even in a crowd. Our lives are so weighted down with the cares of the world that we scarcely can endure life. Our once enchanted hope has faded and feel no one cares.

If this is your plight, know this, you are not alone. Just look around you. Many in the crowd are feeling just like you. You are special and are loved. Look upward and not downward. Your life is important.

There is no right way to do the wrong thing.

Sometimes we rationalize that by doing something wrong is still okay. Doing anything that is "wrong" is never "okay".

Rationalizing something that is wrong can never be considered as right no matter how good, correct, or justified, we believe our motives may be.

We can only live in harmony if we truly love each other. To love someone that we dislike takes a bit of courage and looking for the good in them.

When hate is strong it mocks the song, "peace on Earth goodwill towards men".

Why is there such hatred in the world that it causes people to do awful things towards each other? Is their ideology so strong that it overrules their judgement and morality? It appears so.

Ideology may have supplanted religion. Unlike religion, ideology has no moral basis. It is purely political or economic. There is no "love your neighbor" aspect to it. Therefore, hate supplants love and when this occurs there will be no peace on earth.

Does the presumption of innocence really exist?

While this is a worthy goal, in reality it doesn't work because of bias. What we need to admit is our bias is so strong that the presumption of innocence is impractical. So then how can we deal with the presumption of innocence as a practical matter?

This matter boils down to not jumping to conclusions and taking immediate action. As long as your personal bias does not cause you to take inappropriate action, the presumption of innocence can be a practical matter.

Just count to 10 before reacting.

Hating your enemies will not hurt them but it sure will injure you. Hatred is a horrible and largely self-inflicted disease.

It's interesting and sad to note that the two most popular words in recent memory were "toxic" and "misinformation".

The two most popular words should have been, "gratitude" and "thankfulness".

Compassion is when you take pity on someone. Enlightened compassion is when you not only take pity, but you do something about it.

Anger stems from selfishness. Selfishness stems from greed. This is all a matter of us looking inward and not outward. So how do we focus on being more outward? It is all about being more loving and understanding.

Loving someone is more important than fixing a problem. Yet far too often we are more fixated on problems solving than lending a listening ear to someone in need.

Being compassionate is a better trait than being a good problem solver.

There is a church song that goes, "count your many blessings, name them one by one". A true sign of a gracious and well-founded person is one who is grateful for their many blessings: they don't just take them for granted.

While life can be filled with trials, and these events can bring us down, we live in a beautiful world filled with so many opportunities. The more you focus on the good there is, the happier and more productive your life will be. That is the power of gratitude.

Renown chef committed suicide today.  What is the nature of suicide?

Suicide generally comes about because the individual is extremely unhappy with his or her plight in life. Dealing with mortality and the adversities associated with it is something we all face.

We all have faced challenges that could have been overwhelming. To push on and not give up (committing suicide is a form of 'giving up') requires help from friends and loved ones.

If you know of someone, and it could be you, who is facing challenges, don't assume they can work things out on their own. This can be a huge mistake. Lending an ear or a kind thought might make you the one to save a life.

Stay by their side and help them through the challenge.

"Grasping at straws" means you are trying anything to succeed because nothing you have already tried is working out. It is centered in a feeling of hopelessness, but you just don't want to concede.

So, is grasping at straws a waste of time? It all depends on how you define "trying to succeed". Having the drive to succeed, no matter the obstacles or how hopeless it seems, is the sign of a true optimist.

We all need that faith in order to succeed. Faith involves having hope for, but lacking evidence of things not seen. It is our faith that drives us forward no matter how much the odds are stacked against us.

Be full of hope and faith – ultimately you will beat the odds.

Don't let your wealth of ambition overcome your impoverished lack of experience. Too much ambition can cause us to be overconfident. Overconfidence can make us careless and unwilling to listen and learn. Be confident but humble.

Be a beacon of hope.

During the early days of ocean travel, ports of call would have a beacon to guide the ships safely into the harbor. Without a powerful light to mark the harbor entrance, the ships could end up crashing into shore rather than safely reaching the port.

Without a strong, righteous light to help guide us, we can end up crashing.

We need more people who have the right kind of light to bring us to safety. If you are one of those beacons, or if you are following a beacon, make sure it is the right kind of light that will lead someone safely through ocean of life.

Reverence is more than just being quiet in church. Reverence is holding all things sacred: life, nature, country, leaders, friends, home, marriage, civil servants, teachers, and the list goes on.

Keep reverence in your life and live a happier existence.

My brother recently proposed an interesting suggestion. He said, "may we discover the intended purposes and genuinely seek the welfare of others".

At a time when we have so much animosity and hatred around us, his suggestion touched me deeply. I began to ponder about the "intended purpose" of seeking the welfare of others.

To "seek" means, attempt to find, obtain, desire, or achieve something. Seeking then follows that we earnestly and with all sincerity help others along the pathway of life. The "intended purpose" then, in my mind, is that our success must be hinged to their success.

As they say, "we are all in this together". Can you just imagine that if we all had this fully inculcated in our mind's eye, how much easier and more productive life would be for all of us? I'm in, how about you?

One of the biggest challenges we all face is staying calm, being nice and NEVER snapping out in unkind ways. If we all would develop the counting-to-ten-habit before responding to a situation, we could minimize lashing out in modes that only make things worse.

If you have a habit of making harsh responses, try counting to ten several times a day even if there is no issue that causes you to say something you wished you hadn't. It is good practice, and it works for me.

Dislike, hatred, disrespect, distrust, jealousy and enmity are all rooted in selfishness. These sorts of feelings are what causes the current dilemmas we face in the world today.

We frankly have lost the ability to love others as we love ourselves. We think that everything is all about us and what we want. Where is the concept of being meek and lowly in heart? Doing so puts others first, which requires true strength. It is not being weak and indifferent.

If we can learn and accept that the world is not all about us, we will become more tolerant and understanding of others. When we put other's needs before our own, we minimize the rancor that is permeating our society.

There are a lot of very scary things in life we will face. How we face them is all important.

Franklin D. Roosevelt said, "We have nothing to fear but fear itself". This comment was made during a very difficult period of WW II. But it spoke to not allowing fear to cripple us as a nation. The same applies to us as individuals.

What we don't need is to amplify things to a point where we can hardly move. When we do so, our decision-making ability is also compromised. "Fear" takes control of our lives. We see bogeymen around every corner.

This is where courage comes in. I recall the story of "The Wizard of Oz". In the story, the lion, who you would think wasn't afraid of anything, lacked courage. Courage was the one trait the lion wanted from the Wizard. He was fearful of almost everything. In the end, the Wizard gave the lion a "bravery metal" as recognition of the lion's courage.

If you are fearful and lack courage, you can become less fearful by going outside yourself and serving others.

"Learn from the past and look to the future." This adage says that we should learn from our mistakes and move on. Learning, of course, involves not repeating the same mistake.

Learning starts by gaining knowledge. Wisdom is the proper application of knowledge. For example, we can learn to drive in adverse weather conditions, but we often fail to apply this knowledge when driving in bad weather. This is not wise.

Wisdom alone cannot save us. It is a combination of knowledge and wisdom that provides protection.

Can there ever be a valid reason to injure or defame another person just because we don't like them?

I say NO!" And yet we do this all the time in politics. No wonder politics is considered an ugly game. Some believe that "all is fair in love and war," and apparently, we love the warfare called politics.

Sadly, when it comes to politics, destroying another person or their reputation is considered fair game. Why has this become such an evil necessity? Are politics by nature dirty? Apparently. We can't seem to wage a political campaign without it turning into a dirty fight.

Is it even possible to run a clean political campaign if the opposing side plays dirty? I think so. You may not win an election, but you will certainly lose if you have to wage a dirty campaign. People are by nature "good" and "good" trumps "evil" in the end.

Winning to me involves always being honest with maintaining impeccable integrity.  If you always do the right thing, you are a winner and, in the end, this is what counts.

Why do we hold others to a higher standard than we do ourselves? Is it human nature or just a bad habit? It can be both.

For many people it is their nature to protect themselves by looking for a scape goat. Have you ever noticed that when you have a deficiency or a flaw in yourself that you look to see if others have the same? You feel comforted when you find others equally afflicted. It keeps you from feeling bad or unusual.

One nasty habit is when we require others to not have similar deficiencies or flaws – to be better than ourselves. You may not suffer from the same or similar flaws, but you refuse to allow others to have them. In addition, you might expect certain people, because of who they are or the positions they hold, to not have these imperfections. When we feel this way, it means we are intolerant.

This is ridiculous.

We should not excuse or tolerate actions that are illegal or immoral. Absolutely not! But neither should we be quick to judge. We need to let the proper authorities determine the guilt or innocence. We should not become the judge, jury, and executioner. Just remember, you are not perfect. Cut others some slack.

Without faith, little is possible. But with faith, almost everything is.

Having faith – a belief – is having assurance and confidence in our ability to endure life challenges (or launch a business).

Knowing this, we can see how important faith is in accomplishing goals.

So, if we lack faith and desire to have it, how do we strengthen our faith and benefit from it?  Simply, it is overcoming fear. Fear strangles faith. It is therefore having faith that will belie our fears.

Why do people feel the need to dress in tattered fashion when they have the financial means to do otherwise?

Not so long ago, these kinds of clothes could not be bought in stores. Today you buy "shabby chic" clothes new and off the rack. These ready-made rags actually cost more because the manufacturers spend time trying to make the duds more shabby looking.

No one I know thinks shabby and tattered looks good. So, what is the deal? I have discussed this with younger folk and the simple answer seems to be it is the style. Okay, so let's dig into this "it's the style" meme. How do things become "the style"?

Styles or trends are set by the media; news, social, or entertainment. In the case of shabby and tattered, it was most likely set by the music and entertainment industry. This trend is due to the liberal nature of the music and entertainment industry's desire to promote nonconformity reaching back to the hippy era of the 60's.

There is a danger in such nonconformity. It breeds a lawless attitude toward any kind of structured life. If we recall the 60's, it was fraught with all kinds of problematic experimentation with illicit drugs and sex.  Be very careful about any styles or trends that encourage nonconformity. This can lead to destruction.

This quote comes from my friend, Guy Smith – "Heaven is a place devoid of anger, bitterness, hatred and resentment. Stripped of emotions, people in Heaven can only expose the love within themselves. Heaven on Earth is possible. It starts when you choose to rid yourself of discontent and allow your love to escape and find others."

The gift of being a good "observer" is something we all need to strive for.

To "observe" means to watch for or to perceive something of significance or value. It also means to be respectful, as in observing a worthwhile tradition, holiday or celebration.

The bottom line is that observing is a very worthwhile gift to develop because it shows we are caring, thoughtful, and respectful.

In that famous and stirring song, "The Battle Hymn of the Republic" there is this acclimating chorus, "His truth is marching on".

No matter our religious beliefs, God is in control. This "truth" is undeniable and eternal. No one, no matter how powerful they may believe they are can raise their puny hand in any degree to alter God's plan for us or this great planet on which we live.

This gives me great solace as I ponder and dwell upon all the quagmires and difficulties we are beset with. Know this, God loves His children and is mindful of each and every one of them.

If we only learn through suffering, the entire world would be smarter.

What I believe is we can gain empathy and compassion through the things we suffer but unfortunately, all too often, we become even more hardened.

So why is it that some gain more empathy and others become more hardened through suffering? The simple answer is whether or not we are selfless or selfish.  Focusing on other's needs rather than our own will help us develop a selfless attitude and bring happiness and joy into our lives.

I find it hard to believe that all life began without the help of a divine creator.

If you look at all animal life, they all have basically the same organs, a heart, brain, lungs, liver, kidneys, digestive system, reproductive system, etc. This, to me, means that all life is divine and should be treated with dignity and respect and yet we don't seem to treat each other, whether human or not, with dignity and respect.

It may be this lack of belief in a divine creator that causes the world, as a whole, not to treat all life well. I throw this thought out for all to consider, whether religious or not, that we believe all life as precious and deserving of respect just in case there is a divine creator, and we might just be held accountable for any mistreatment and disregard of life.

Failing to love others is loving to fail.

Without love in our lives, we are the most miserable of humanity. It is love that keeps us on the straight and narrow, doing what is right. It is love that leads us to be kind, empathetic, non-judgmental, forgiving.

Love is the driving force that keeps society stable and peaceful. It is at this juncture, with all the hate and strife that exists, that we need more love and compassion.

Don't fail to love but overcome the failure of not being more loving.

# About Ray Zinn

Raymond D. "Ray" Zinn is an inventor, entrepreneur, and the longest serving CEO of a publicly traded company in Silicon Valley.

Zinn is known best for conceptualizing and in effect inventing the Wafer Stepper, and for co-founding semiconductor company Micrel (acquired by Microchip in 2015), which provides essential components for smartphones, consumer electronics and enterprise networks. He has served as Chief Executive Officer, Chairman of its Board of Directors and President since the Company's inception in 1978.

Zinn led Micrel profitably through eight major downturns in global chip markets, an impressive achievement. Many chip companies weren't able to make it through one downturn and very few have survived through all the major downturns. Micrel has been profitable from its very first year, aside from one year during the dot-com implosion.

Ray Zinn holds over 20 patents for semiconductor design. He has been mentioned in several books, including Jim Fixx's The Complete Book of Running and Essentialism by Greg McKeown.

* 9 7 9 8 7 3 7 2 9 1 9 3 8 *